P9-DBH-959

GREAT SPORTS TEAMS

THE SAN FRANCISCO 49ERS

Other Books in the Great Sports Teams Series:

The Dallas Cowboys
The Los Angeles Lakers
The New York Yankees

GREAT SPORTS TEAMS

THE SAN FRANCISCO 49ERS

JOHN F. GRABOWSKI

Lucent Books, San Diego, CA

On cover: Charlie Garner carrying the ball.

Library of Congress Cataloging-in-Publication Data

RM TH

Grabowski, John F.
The San Francisco 49ers / by John F. Grabowski.
p. cm. — (Great sports teams)
Includes bibliographical references and index.
Summary: Discusses the history, formation, and development of The San Francisco 49ers football team, featuring such players as Joe Perry, Hugh McElhenny, Bill Walsh, Joe Montana, Ronnie Lott, Jerry Rice, and Steve Young.
ISBN 1-56006-947-3 (hardback : alk. paper)
1. San Francisco 49ers (Football team)—Juvenile literature. [1. San Francisco 49ers (Football team)—History. 2. Football—History.] I. Title II. Series
GV956.S3 G715 2002
796.332'64'0979461—dc21

10911 Technology Place, San Diego, 92127

Printed in the U.S.A.

21,95

Contents

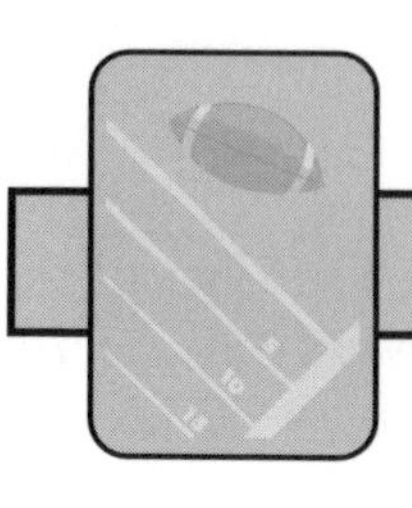

FOREWORD

Former Supreme Court Chief Justice Warren Burger once said he always read the sports section of the newspaper first because it was about humanity's successes, while the front page listed only humanity's failures. Millions of people across the country today would probably agree with Burger's preference for tales of human endurance, record-breaking performances, and feats of athletic prowess. Although these accomplishments are far beyond what most Americans can ever hope to achieve, average people, the fans, do want to affect what happens on the field of play. Thus, their role becomes one of encouragement. They cheer for their favorite players and team and boo the opposition.

ABC Sports president Roone Arledge once attempted to explain the relationship between fan and team. Sport, said Arledge, is "a set of created circumstances—artificial circumstances—set up to frustrate a man in pursuit of a goal. He has to have certain skills to overcome those obstacles—or even to challenge them. And people who don't have those skills cheer him and admire him." Over a period of time, the admirers may develop a rabid—even irrational—allegiance to a particular team. Indeed, the word "fan" itself is derived from the word "fanatic," someone possessed by an excessive and irrational zeal. Sometimes this devotion to a team is because of a favorite player; often it's because of where a person lives, and, occasionally, it's because of a family allegiance to a particular club.

Whatever the reason, the bond formed between team and fan often defies reason. It may be easy to understand the appeal of the New York Yankees, a team that has gone to the World Series an incredible thirty-eight times and won twenty-six championships, nearly three times as many as any other major league baseball team. It is more difficult, though, to comprehend the fanaticism of Chicago Cubs fans, who faithfully follow the progress of a team that hasn't won a World Series since 1908. Regardless, the Cubs have surpassed the 2 million mark in home attendance in fourteen of the last seventeen years. In fact, their two highest totals were posted in 1999 and 2000, when the team finished in last place.

Each volume in Lucent's *Great Sports Teams in History* series examines a team that has left its mark on the "American sports consciousness." Each book looks at the history and tradition of the club in an attempt to understand its appeal and the loyalty—even passion—of its fans. Each volume also examines the lives and careers of people who played significant roles in the team's history. Players, managers, coaches, and front-office executives are represented.

Endnoted quotations help bring the text in each book to life. In addition, all books include an annotated bibliography and a For Further Reading list to supply students with sources for conducting additional individual research.

No one volume can hope to explain fully the mystique of the New York Yankees, Boston Celtics, Dallas Cowboys, or Montreal Canadiens. The Lucent *Great Sports Teams in History* series, however, gives interested readers a solid start on the road to understanding the mysterious bond that exists between modern professional sports teams and their devoted followers.

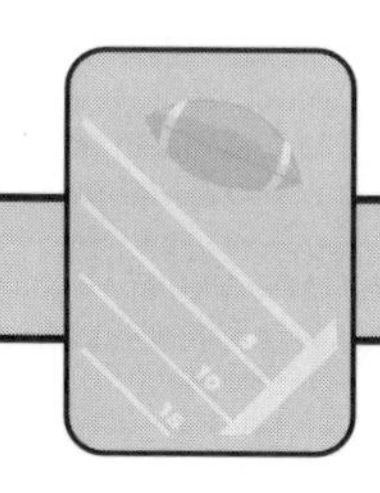

INTRODUCTION

Filling a Void

The San Francisco 49ers came into existence in 1946 as a charter member of the All-America Football Conference (AAFC), a new professional league formed to compete with the National Football League (NFL). The 49ers are the longest continuously running franchise to be located on the West Coast in any of the four major team sports. By giving the fans an exciting, winning club, owner Anthony Morabito showed that the Bay Area was ready and able to support a professional sports team. The 49ers are one of the most successful teams in the history of professional football and have a tradition of which their fans can be justly proud.

The Merger

In 1950 the AAFC disbanded and the NFL agreed to absorb the Baltimore Colts, Cleveland Browns, and San Francisco 49ers into the older, established circuit. Of the three teams, only the 49ers have remained in continuous residence in their original city. In a day and age when franchise shifts are not all that unusual, San Francisco fans have supported their club for more than a half century, whether it be at Kezar Stadium or Candlestick Park (renamed 3Com Park in 1995). They have been rewarded for their loyalty with entertaining, competitive championship teams.

The team was the dream of one man—Anthony J. Morabito. That dream depended on the support of the fans of the Bay Area in order to be a success. That they have done so is a testament to both the city and the team. The love affair between San Francisco and the 49ers continues strong after more than half a century. This mutual affection was demonstrated by former 49er owner Eddie DeBartolo.

In 1946, their debut year, the San Francisco 49ers hand the Cleveland Browns their first loss of the season.

After stepping down as owner, he ran a full-page message in the *San Francisco Chronicle*. In it he thanked the city and its fans for their graciousness to him and his family and for their support. Such a public acknowledgment is almost unheard of, but indicative of the relationship that exists between the 49ers and their fans.

Both sides benefit from this affiliation, with pro football being the biggest winner of all. For five decades, 49ers legends like Hugh McElhenny, Joe Montana, and Jerry Rice have thrilled fans with record-breaking performances. They are part of a tradition that has made the San Francisco 49ers one of the most successful sports franchises of the recent past.

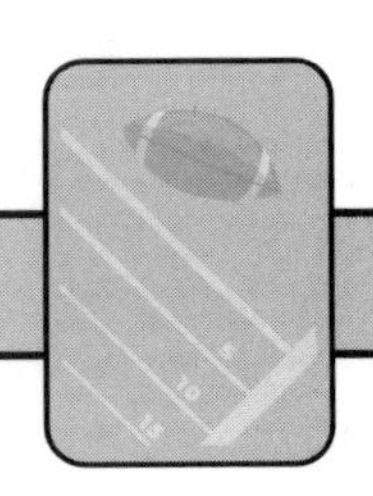

CHAPTER 1

Excitement Personified

Over the years some National Football League teams have become synonymous with outstanding defensive play. Super Bowl clubs have been built around defensive units such as the Purple People Eaters (Minnesota Vikings), the Steel Curtain (Pittsburgh Steelers), and the Doomsday Defense (Dallas Cowboys).

The San Francisco 49ers, on the other hand, have earned a reputation for explosive play and offensive innovations. The Million Dollar Backfield, the Alley-Oop Pass, the Shotgun Formation, and the West Coast Offense have helped make the 49ers one of the most fun teams in the league to watch. Offensive stars such as Joe "the Jet" Perry, Hugh "the King" McElhenny, Joe Montana, Jerry Rice, and Steve Young have left their marks on the NFL record book. The appeal of their wide-open style of play is reflected by the team's status as one of the league's most successful franchises, both on the field and at the box office.

A Man of Great Vision

Anthony J. "Tony" Morabito was a San Francisco lumber executive with a dream—to bring professional football to the San Francisco area. At the time (the early 1940s), there were no NFL teams west of Chicago. Morabito approached the league with a request for a franchise in 1941. He was turned down because of the popularity of college football teams in the region. A new team, the NFL reasoned, would not draw well with such competition. In addition, the travel costs involved for teams coming to play in San Francisco would be exorbitant. Morabito was disappointed but did not give up hope. He continued his efforts over the years, but NFL commissioner Elmer Layden turned a deaf ear to his pleas.

In the spring of 1944, Morabito heard news that caught his attention. Arch Ward—the sports editor of the *Chicago Tribune* and the man responsible for starting baseball's All-Star Game—was trying to establish a new professional football league to compete with the NFL. Morabito contacted Ward and was invited to the first meeting of the All-America Football Conference (AAFC). On June 6, 1944, his dream finally came true. The first major sports league team on the West Coast came into existence as the San Francisco club was granted charter membership in the AAFC after posting a $25,000 admittance fee. The league made plans to begin play in 1946.

The All-America Football Conference—Year One

Morabito proved to be a visionary. The Bay Area was at the start of a postwar building boom, and as former business partner Al Ruffo said, "It was just the right time."[1] Morabito enlisted two other business acquaintances—Allen E. Sorrell and Ernest J. Turre—together with his younger brother, Victor, to become partners in the franchise. It was Sorrell, reportedly, who came up with the name 49ers to honor the pioneers who came to northern California during the gold rush of 1849 and eventually helped establish the city of San Francisco.

Morabito's next order of business was to hire a coach for his team. He settled on Lawrence "Buck" Shaw, the former head coach at Stanford University. The hiring of the well-respected Shaw gave the team—and the league—immediate respectability. Morabito then went about getting players under contract. He concentrated on those who had played their college ball in the Bay Area, knowing they would attract local fans. Among the players signed were quarterback Frankie Albert, fullback Norman Standlee, and guard Bruno Banducci of Stanford, and end Alyn Beals of Santa Clara.

Coach Buck Shaw (right) instructs Frankie Albert (center) and Norm Standlee (left), the first additions to Morabito's 49ers.

By the time the 49ers were ready to play their first exhibition game, the organization had already laid out a staggering $250,000 for basics such as uniforms, equipment, and so on. As Ruffo said, "Everything was first-class. Tony wanted everything first-class all the time."[2]

The 49ers took the field for the first time in an exhibition game against the Los Angeles Dons on August 24, 1946, at Balboa Park in San Diego. Only eight thousand people showed up to see the 49ers come out on top by a score of 17–7. They fared better at the gate in their first home game at Kezar Stadium in San Francisco the following week. More than forty thousand fans turned out to see San Francisco defeat the Chicago Rockets, 34–14. The victory impressed many members of the media. *Chronicle* sports editor Bill Leiser gushed, "Their team, we think, is as good as any professional team we ever saw, including the best of the Chicago Bear teams. It is much better than the present National League Champion Los Angeles Rams team."[3]

The 49ers drew nearly thirty-six thousand people to their season opener against the New York Yankees. San Francisco scored first on a 66-yard pass and lateral. It was a harbinger of the type of wide-open, imaginative style of play the team would become known for in the years to come.

The Yankees bounced back to win the opener, 21–7, but the 49ers won nine of their remaining thirteen games to finish their maiden season in second place in the Western Division. Professional football was a success in its debut in the City by the Bay.

An Exciting Team

Morabito did his best to draw fans to 49er games and to provide exciting entertainment for those fans. Following the team's first season, he made headlines when he tried to sign Army's "Touchdown Twins," Glenn Davis and Doc Blanchard. Although he was unsuccessful, he did sign pro football's first Asian American player, speedy Wally Yonamine from Honolulu, Hawaii. Despite not having played college ball, Yonamine helped the team to an 8-4-2 record in 1947 and another second-place finish. The year also saw San Francisco unveil its fancy new red-and-gold uniforms.

For 1948 the 49ers added fullback Joe Perry and end Hal Shoener to their already explosive attack. The results were spectacular with the team setting several offensive records. The 49ers averaged 5 touchdowns a game and 6.5 yards per carry for the year. Quarterback Albert threw for 2,104 yards and 29 touchdowns as he led the team to a 12-2 mark.

The next year, the AAFC's fourth and final season, San Francisco finally made it to the playoffs. The 49ers defeated the Yankees, then moved on to the league Championship Game against the Cleveland Browns. Two days prior to the game, it was announced that the All-America Football Conference had merged with the National Football League. Three AAFC teams—San Francisco, Cleveland, and Baltimore—would be joining the older, established league for the 1950 season. On December 11, 1949, the Browns defeated the 49ers, 21–7, in the final game in AAFC history.

Hoisting coach Paul Brown in the air, Cleveland players celebrate their victory in the final game in AAFC history.

On to the NFL

The 49ers struggled in their first NFL season. In the team's very first game, they were soundly beaten by a mediocre Washington Redskins squad, 31–14. As Bill Leiser wrote, "Frankly, they did not look capable of beating any team in the National Football League."[4] San Francisco finished the year with just three wins in twelve games.

The team improved quickly, however, adding quarterback Y. A. Tittle and end Billy Wilson for the 1951 season and halfback Hugh McElhenny the next year. It did not take McElhenny long to become a fan favorite, with his breakaway speed and broken-field runs. He was a threat to score any time he touched the ball, be it on a run, pass, kickoff return, or punt return.

The 49ers continued their exciting play despite a growing quarterback controversy. Tittle eventually took over the bulk of the playing time, with Frankie Albert seeing occasional action. McElhenny's running partner, fullback Joe Perry, ground out yards with punishing regularity. He rushed for over 1,000 yards in both 1953 and 1954. In the latter year, running back John Henry Johnson joined the team following a trade with the Pittsburgh Steelers. He was the final piece of the most lethal backfield combination of the mid-1950s. The quartet of Tittle, McElhenny, Perry, and Johnson became known far and wide as the Million Dollar Backfield, a title given to them by team publicist Dan McGuire in an attempt to generate publicity. (In truth, the salaries of the four players totaled less than $100,000.)

The exciting 49er offense made the team a favorite with fans around the league as well as with those in San Francisco. They came out in droves to see one of the league's most potent attacks. In a 1957 game against the Rams in the Los Angeles Coliseum, an NFL-record 102,368 fans filled the stands to watch the home team send the 49ers down to defeat, 37–24.

That season also saw end R. C. Owens make his debut. Owens teamed up with Tittle to make the Alley-Oop Pass an important, exciting new weapon in the 49ers' arsenal. In the Alley-Oop, Tittle threw the ball high in Owens's direction. The former College of Idaho basketball star used his extraordinary leaping ability to outjump opposing defenders and make the catch.

Unfortunately, 1957 was also a season of tragedy. San Francisco owner Tony Morabito died in the stands during a 49er game against the Chicago Bears on October 27. Although the club bounced back to finish the year tied for the Western Conference title, they lost a playoff game to the Detroit Lions. It would be more than a decade before the team would see postseason action again.

Mediocrity

The 49ers struggled through the next dozen years, the leanest period in the club's history. The team would not win more than seven games in any season from 1958 through 1969, despite the best efforts of head coaches Red Hickey, Jack Christiansen, and Dick Nolan.

Despite San Francisco's lackluster performance, it was still a fun team to watch. In 1960 Hickey unveiled the new Shotgun Formation during a game with the Baltimore Colts. In the Shotgun, the quarterback stood several yards behind the center to take the snap. By doing so, he had more room in which to maneuver, and more time to assess the options available to him.

The following off-season, the club drafted quarterback Billy Kilmer from the University of California at Los Angeles (UCLA). Kilmer was the perfect man for the Shotgun—a skillful passer as well as an above-average runner. He shared time with John Brodie (until moving on to the New Orleans Saints in 1967), throwing to one of the league's best corps of receivers, which included Dave Parks, Bernie Casey, and Monty Stickles.

By 1965 the 49ers' attack had become more rounded. Fullback Ken Willard and former Heisman Trophy winner John David Crow solidified the running game. San Francisco averaged more than 30 points a contest that year, scoring a franchise-record 52 against the Chicago Bears in the opening game of the season. Unfortunately, the defense had difficulty holding the opposition. When the 49ers played the Bears a second time, in the middle of December, Chicago came out on top by a score of 61–20.

Highs and Lows

For the six-year period from 1962 to 1967, the 49er defense surrendered an average of more than 25 points per contest. It was obvious that this part of their game needed to improve significantly for the team to take the next step and reach title contender status. In 1968 the team hired defensive expert Dick Nolan to help them.

By 1970 the club was ready to make a run at the title. All-Pros Dave Wilcox at linebacker and Jimmy Johnson at defensive back fortified a steadily improving defense. Defensive back Bruce Taylor was named Rookie of the Year; quarterback Brodie, the

National Football Conference (NFC) Player of the Year; and Nolan, the NFC Coach of the Year. The 49ers went all the way to the NFC Championship Game for the first time in their history but lost to the Dallas Cowboys.

The 49ers made it back to the NFC Championship Game before again losing to Dallas in 1971. The next season they met the Cowboys once more, this time in the first round of the playoffs. The

Guided by Roger Staubach, the Cowboys celebrate a miraculous comeback victory over the 49ers.

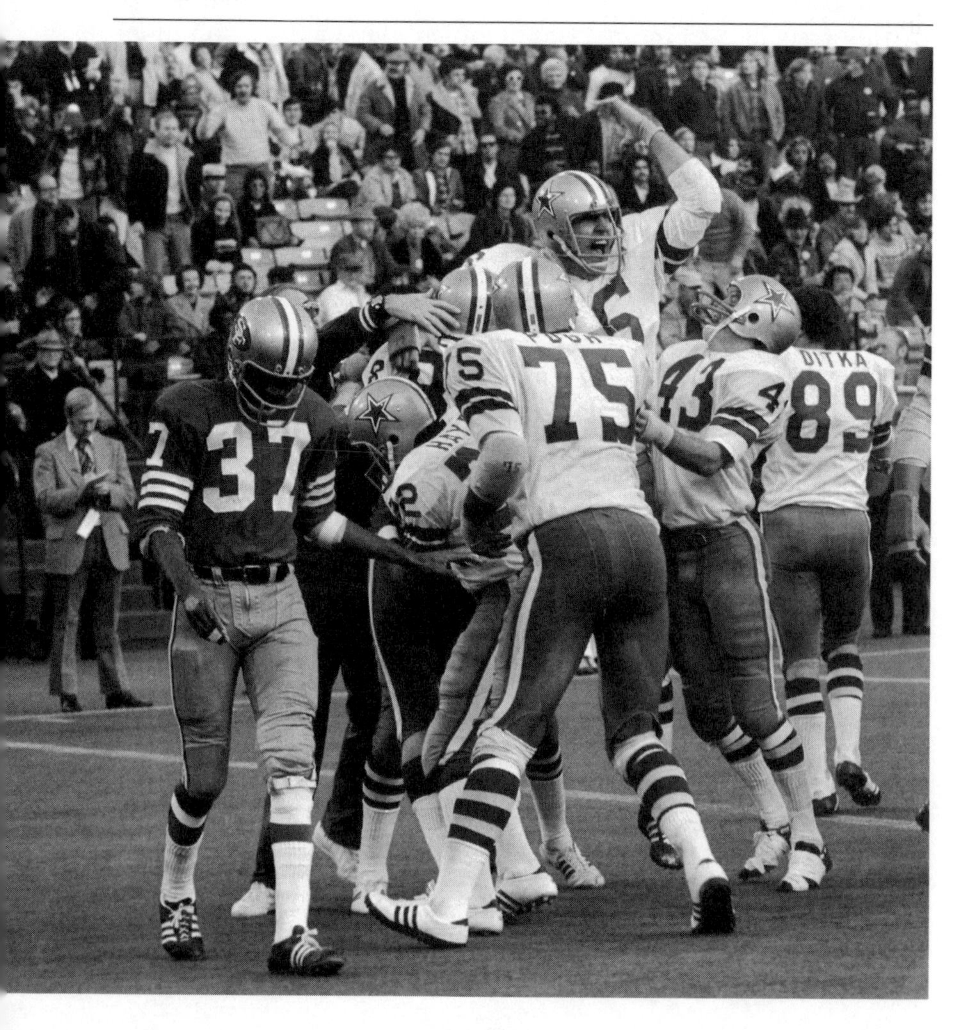

49ers led, 28–13, with just nine minutes left in the game when Dallas coach Tom Landry replaced quarterback Craig Morton with Roger Staubach. Staubach guided the Cowboys to a miraculous comeback and a 30–28 win, ending San Francisco's season for the third consecutive year. The 49ers found it difficult to bounce back from the devastating loss. They finished in last place in 1973 and did not post a winning record again until 1976.

Prior to the start of the 1977 season, the Morabito family sold the 49ers to Edward DeBartolo Jr. The change in ownership did not halt the team's slide. San Francisco hit rock bottom in 1978, compiling a 2-14 record. Better days, however, were on the horizon.

The Bill Walsh Era

Before the start of the 1979 season, the 49ers made two moves that had a dramatic effect on the team's future. First, DeBartolo hired former Stanford University coach Bill Walsh as head coach and general manager. Second, Walsh selected quarterback Joe Montana from Notre Dame in the third round of the 1979 college draft.

Although the changes did not immediately translate into victories, a difference could be seen on the field. After finishing last in most offensive categories the previous season, the 49ers produced one of the league's most potent attacks in 1979. The defense, unfortunately, was still one of the league's worst.

The decade of the eighties began with Montana easing his way into a starting role. End Dwight Clark, selected in the same 1979 draft, became the team's leading receiver. The defense was improved with the selection of Ronnie Lott, Eric Wright, and Carlton Williamson in the 1981 draft, and the acquisition of Jack Reynolds and Fred Dean through trades. The result was a Super Bowl championship in 1981, the first title in any major sport for the City by the Bay and the start of one of the greatest runs by any team in NFL history. In the eighteen-year stretch from 1981 through 1998, the 49ers would have seventeen seasons with at least ten wins, make the playoffs sixteen times, win thirteen Western Division crowns, and be triumphant in five Super Bowls.

Walsh's offense added a new dimension in 1983 with the addition of rookie fullback Roger Craig and halfback Wendell Tyler. The next year, with a running game that nicely complemented its passing attack, the 49ers put together one of the greatest seasons in

NFL history. The team lost just one game all year on the way to another championship in Super Bowl XIX.

Walsh's West Coast Offense (a system dependent on quick, short, high-percentage passes) got a boost with the addition of wide receiver Jerry Rice in the 1985 college draft, but Craig was the player who stole the show. The versatile fullback rushed for 1,050 yards and added 1,106 more yards on receptions, thus becoming the first player in league history to top the 1,000-yard mark both ways in the same season.

The second half of the decade saw Rice emerge as the premiere wide receiver in the NFL. His 22 touchdown receptions in 1987 set a new league mark, and Montana won the first passing title of his career. The next year Craig rushed for 1,502 yards to set a new San Francisco record. Rice starred in the playoffs, winning the Most

Coach Walsh, quarterback Montana, and owner DeBartolo hold the Super Bowl XIX trophy from one of the greatest seasons in NFL history.

Valuable Player Award for Super Bowl XXIII in Walsh's final year as head coach.

Seifert Takes Over

George Seifert was named to succeed Walsh in 1989, and the 49ers did not miss a beat. Fourth-year fullback Tom Rathman led NFC running backs with 73 receptions, adding a new wrinkle to the league's best attack. Montana, Rice, and Craig were their usual brilliant selves as the 49ers again went to the Super Bowl. There, they beat the Denver Broncos, winning by a score of 55–10. The victory made San Francisco the first team to repeat as champions since the 1978–79 Pittsburgh Steelers.

The 49ers seemed on track for another Super Bowl in 1990 following an NFL-best 14-2 record in the regular season. An injury to Joe Montana in the NFC Championship Game, however, ruined their chances and kept him out of action for most of the next two seasons.

Steve Young was given his chance to run the team, bringing a different look to the San Francisco offense. In addition to his pinpoint passing accuracy, he was a threat any time he had the ball. In 1992 the 49ers added running back Ricky Watters, who established a new team rushing record for rookies with 1,013 yards on the ground.

When Montana returned to action in the last regular season game that year, it raised the question of who would guide the team in 1993. The question was answered when the aging Montana was sent to the Kansas City Chiefs prior to the start of the season. Without having to worry about the legendary Montana looking over his shoulder, Young led the NFL in passing for the third straight season. The 49ers led the league in both scoring and total offense, but for the second year in a row, lost to the Dallas Cowboys in the NFC Championship Game.

San Francisco owner Eddie DeBartolo bolstered the club's defense the next year, signing free agents Deion Sanders, Ken Norton Jr., Gary Plummer, and Rickey Jackson. The newcomers sparked the team to another Western Division title. With Young and wide receiver Jerry Rice starring, the 49ers scored a franchise-record 505 points. They then steamrolled through the playoffs on the way to their record-setting fifth Super Bowl win in Super Bowl XXIX.

Head coach George Seifert (center) watches as the 49ers defeat the San Diego Chargers in Super Bowl XXIX.

The 49ers continued to post winning records and make appearances in the playoffs. George Seifert, under whom the team won two Super Bowls, retired following the 1995 season. He left with the highest winning percentage in NFL history (.755), on the basis of a 108-35 record.

A Change at the Top

San Francisco maintained its winning ways under new coach Steve Mariucci. The 49ers won in double figures in 1996, 1997, and 1998. However, they fell short of reaching the Super Bowl each year. Running back Garrison Hearst took over as the team's leading rusher, gaining a 49er-record 1,570 yards in 1998. The 49ers, however, were starting to show their age. Injuries, free agency, and poor drafts were beginning to take a toll.

Adding to the problems were the suspension of owner Eddie DeBartolo because of his involvement in gambling, a feud between DeBartolo and his sister—Denise DeBartolo York—for control of the team, and the return (and subsequent departure) of Bill Walsh in a general manager capacity. San Francisco suffered through its worst season in twenty years in 1999, finishing at 4-12. An injury to Young forced him into an early retirement and left the team without a proven quarterback. Jeff Garcia took over and showed promise for the future. The defense, however, struggled and salary-cap restrictions made it impossible for the 49ers to compete for free agents who might help the team.

As the millennium came to a close, the 49ers were forced to face the fact that the dynasty of the past quarter century was finished. Its extraordinary run of success is not likely to be matched by any team in the immediate future. What is certain, however, is that the fans of San Francisco will continue to be treated to entertaining football as they support their club and hold tight to the memories of a remarkable past.

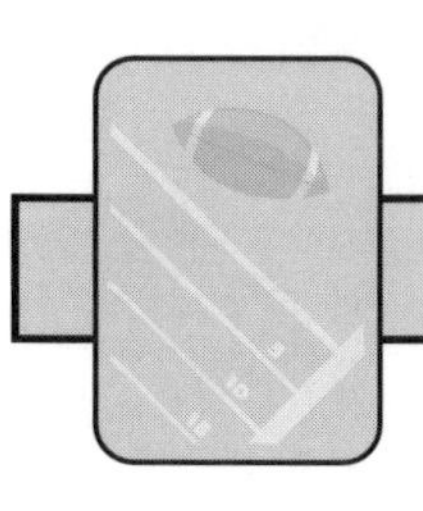

Chapter 2

Joe Perry

Joe Perry was one of the few blacks in professional football in the late 1940s and early 1950s. As such, he faced obstacles similar to those faced by Jackie Robinson when he broke baseball's color line. Perry overcame those obstacles and, using his speed and power, went on to become one of the top fullbacks of his day and a rushing champion in both the All-America Football Conference and the National Football League.

An All-Around Athlete

Fletcher Joseph Perry was born in Stevens, Arkansas, on January 27, 1927, the second child (after daughter Louella) of Fletcher Lee and Laurah Perry. His maternal grandparents were black, while his grandparents on his father's side were part Cherokee and Blackfoot Indian. Joe's dad worked in the mines near Stevens until he was severely burned in an accident when Joe was an infant. As a result, the family moved to southern California, where his father eventually got a job in a tin plant.

Growing up in southern California, Joe was taught by his parents to stand up for his beliefs. He never backed down from anyone, a trait he acquired from his dad. "[My dad] didn't take anything from anybody, black, white or green," remembered Joe. "I got my backbone from my dad. I got integrity from my dad. And I got my fairness with people from my dad."[5]

Joe was an excellent student in school, with mathematics being his best subject. He planned on becoming an electrical engineer when he got older. Sports were secondary with him until high school. At David Starr Jordan High School in Los Angeles, Joe became involved in baseball and basketball. He also starred in track and field, running the 100- and 200-yard dashes, high jumping, broad jumping, and throwing the shot put.

Knowing his mother did not want him participating in football, which she considered a dangerous sport, Joe decided to forge her signature on the parental permission form. Mrs. Perry found out, however, when he hurt himself the very first day of practice. Much to his surprise, she allowed him to continue playing. As Joe ex-

Joe Perry (34) overcame professional football's color line, becoming one of the top fullbacks of his time.

plained, "She figured if I wanted something that badly, why stop me?"[6]

Perry quickly became the star of the team, winning the starting tailback job as a freshman. He was named third-team all-city that year, dominating play with his running, passing, punting, and placekicking. He continued to build on his success in the remaining three years of high school.

When it came time to select a college, Joe's first choice was the UCLA. Unfortunately, he was snubbed by the school's football coach and enrolled at Compton Junior College instead. It was there that he scored 22 touchdowns in 1944.

Joe's education was interrupted the next year by World War II. At the age of seventeen, he enlisted in the navy and served in the Pacific. At the conclusion of the fighting, he was stationed in San Francisco, where he completed his tour of duty at the Alameda Naval Air Station.

While at Alameda, Perry's refusal to back down when he felt he was wronged got him into trouble. Jewel Brown, whom he had met at Compton and eventually married, was due to give birth to their child. Joe requested an extended pass so that he could be with his wife for the birth, but he was denied. Furious, he left anyway. When he returned, he was given a deck court-martial, which was nearly as serious as a dishonorable discharge.

Despite the unfortunate incident, Joe played softball and football for the Alameda Naval Air Station Hellcats, right across the bay from San Francisco. While there, he was noticed by 49er tackle John Woudenberg. Woudenberg recommended the hard-nosed Perry to San Francisco owner Tony Morabito, who signed him for the team. Over time a strong kinship developed between the pair. "Tony loved Joe," remembered former 49er general manager Lou Spadia. "Joe was his favorite player."[7] Perry and Morabito even developed an unusual business relationship. "The whole time I played for Tony," said Joe, "I never knew what I made. I never signed a contract. I had that kind of trust in Tony, and he always took care of me."[8]

The Jet Takes Off

It was during a preseason practice in Perry's rookie season of 1948 that he was given his nickname—"the Jet"—by Frankie Albert because of his explosive starts. "Frankie called a quick trap," recalled Perry. "He took the snap, turned, and I was already by him. He said to someone, 'Perry is just like one of those big jets that come by here.'"[8]

The Jet made an impressive debut with San Francisco. In the opening game of the 1948 AAFC season, the 49ers played the Buffalo Bills. The very first time he touched the ball, Perry raced 58 yards for a touchdown. He gained a total of 65 yards in 3 carries for a 21.6-yard average.

That year the Jet shot through opposing defenses for an average of 7.3 yards per carry as a rookie. During one stretch in the season, he scored touchdowns in nine consecutive games, despite seeing limited action. By the end of the year, he had taken over the starting fullback position from local favorite Norm Standlee.

Perry was a powerful runner. He could run over defenders or drag them along behind him. In addition to opposing defenses, he had other adversities to face, especially in his early years. As one of the few black players in professional football, he was subjected to racism both on and off the field. "There were a lot of unpleasant things that happened," said Perry. "Lots of things were said on the field. You could imagine what they were. It was probably worse playing football instead of baseball . . . because football is such a physical game."[9]

As a running back, Perry was often at the bottom of piles, where bodies hid him from the view of the officials. He was kicked, punched, and elbowed by those who resented playing on the same field as a black man. Perry responded in the way his parents had taught him. He did not go looking for trouble, but he did not back down when challenged. He stood up for himself at all times. "I didn't hear racial slurs from every team," he recalled. "But I heard them until I got respect. Then it was like, 'This guy can play. I can't intimidate him.' After that, we got along."[10]

Despite the racial attitudes of many of the players of the day, in later years Perry had nothing but praise for his former 49er teammates. "The 49ers were great," he said. "If one person was in a fight, the whole team was in a fight. We were like a big family. That was a part of the Morabito influence."[11] For several of his years with San Francisco, Perry even had a white roommate, named, ironically enough, Verl Lillywhite. Lillywhite had attended Modesto Junior College and had played against Perry in school. "We had a lot of fun together," said Joe about their days as roommates. "Verl was more like a brother to me."[12]

A New League

Perry followed up his rookie season by leading the AAFC in rushing in 1949. He had some of his biggest games against the Cleveland Browns, by far the strongest team in the league. In 1949 San Francisco handed Cleveland its worst defeat in the franchise's existence. Perry scored a pair of touchdowns in the 56–28 rout, and rushed for 156 yards in just 16 carries, or an average of nearly 10 yards per carry.

The league folded that year, however, and the 49ers were accepted into the National Football League for the 1950 season. The switch of leagues did not bother Perry. He sparkled in the 49ers' first NFL victory, racing for 142 yards on 16 carries against the Baltimore Colts. Perry finished the year fifth in the league in rushing, though the 49ers struggled to a 3-9 mark.

With Perry running the ball even more than before, the next few years saw the 49ers become one of the better teams in the Western Conference of the NFL. Fellow running back Hugh McElhenny appreciated Perry's all-around talent. "He was such an outstanding team player," he said. "Running backs are only as good as the guys in front of them. I don't know how many times he laid a block that sprang me. I'm just proud to say I was in the same backfield as him."[13]

Perry still, however, had to struggle with racism. In 1952 the 49ers stayed in San Antonio, Texas, for an exhibition game. While his teammates stayed in a hotel, Perry was forced to stay in a room in a private home. As McElhenny recalled, "After that, we'd sit and talk for long hours on the black-and-white problem. Joe used to say, 'I stay in the game to better my race.'"[14]

Perry did not let racism affect his performance on the field. His breakthrough year was 1953, when he rushed for a league-leading total of 1,018 yards. He also led the league in touchdowns with 13, including 3 on pass receptions. In appreciation of his performance, Morabito rewarded him with a $5,090 bonus—$5 for every rushing yard. Following the season, Perry was named to the first-team All-Pro squad for the first time in his career.

The next year Perry raced for 1,049 yards, making him the first player ever to surpass the 1,000-yard plateau in two consecutive years. He demonstrated his range of football skills when he was asked to substitute for injured placekicker Gordy Soltau. Perry was successful on six of seven points after touchdown attempts and one of three field goal attempts. "Because I had a strong leg," said Perry, "the coaches wanted me to kick. I did it for a while, but I told them I was too tired from running the ball to also have to kick. They finally listened to me."[15]

A Special Honor

Because of Perry's outstanding 1954 season and his value to the team, Tony Morabito planned a special honor for Perry. On August 28, 1955, he held Joe Perry Day at Kezar Stadium prior to San Francisco's preseason game with the Cleveland Browns. It was the first

Laying a block that sprang quarterback Frankie Albert (63), Joe Perry (74) demonstrates an unmatched team attitude.

such day ever to honor a black football star, and Joe had fond memories of the occasion. "I was a favorite son," recalled Perry. "They named some street after me in San Francisco. . . . It was a great day on Joe Perry Day. I got TV sets and a lot of stuff for the house."[16]

The 1955 season, unfortunately, turned out to be a forgettable one. San Francisco head coach Buck Shaw had been fired after the 1954 season, and Norman "Red" Strader replaced him. The players did not respond well to Strader's strict discipline, particularly after Shaw's more relaxed style. The team dropped to 4-8 when Perry

Frankie Albert's relaxed approach to football was a welcome change for Perry.

suffered a knee injury and missed only his second game in eight professional seasons. However, Strader was fired after one season and was replaced by former 49er quarterback Frankie Albert. The change was welcomed by Perry. "Frankie was fun to play for," said Joe. "He told me that if I didn't take him out with me after games, he'd fine me."[17]

A Bittersweet Season

The 49ers showed some improvement under Albert, finishing 5-6-1 in 1956. With Hugh McElhenny taking over a larger part of the rushing load, Perry rushed for only 520 yards, the lowest total of his career to that point.

Although San Francisco improved to 8-4 the next year, 1957 proved to be a tough season for the team. On October 27, the 49ers trailed the Chicago Bears, 17–7, after two quarters. During halftime they received the news that Tony Morabito, their beloved owner and Perry's close friend, had suffered a heart attack during the game and died. As Perry recalled, "We saw the medics going up to the press box. We knew it was Tony because he had had heart problems. . . . I hadn't played much that day. I told Frankie at halftime I wanted to go in because of Tony."[18]

Perry rushed for only 11 yards on 4 carries that day. "I was playing in the game and crying at the same time," said Joe. "From the time we first met, Tony and I were like father and son, and it was like losing my father."[19] The 49ers managed to hold Chicago scoreless in the second half and came back to defeat the Bears, 21–17.

With Tony's death, his younger brother Vic assumed control of the team. After suffering three straight defeats in November, the 49ers' record stood at 7-4 heading into the last week of the season. San Francisco needed a victory over the Green Bay Packers to clinch a tie for the Western Conference title with the Detroit Lions. At halftime the outlook was bleak for the 49ers, as Green Bay held a 20–10 lead. In the second half, however, Perry scored on two touchdown runs and San Francisco won by a score of 27–20.

A game to determine the conference winner was played in San Francisco on December 22, 1957. More than sixty thousand fans showed up to see the 49ers gain a 27–7 lead in the third quarter. A first-ever appearance in the NFL Championship Game seemed all but assured. During halftime, however, the Lions had heard the

49ers do some premature celebrating in their locker room. Fired up, they mounted a furious comeback and eked out a 31–27 win. A season that had begun with high hopes ended with the team's most difficult loss ever.

Perry's rushing figures continued to drop in 1957. He gained only 454 yards on the ground as injuries limited his playing time to just eight games. To some it might have appeared that his career was over. Joe, however, felt otherwise. He bounced back in 1958, at age thirty-one, to gain 758 yards and finish third in the league in rushing. Included among his efforts was a career-high 174-yard game against the Lions. He raced for a 73-yard touchdown that day and averaged an incredible 13.4 yards on each of his 13 carries.

A Bitter Parting of the Ways

Perry's performance in the 1958 season proved he could still play at a high level, in spite of his advancing age. New San Francisco head coach Howard "Red" Hickey, however, saw things differently. Hickey began to use running back J. D. Smith more frequently, phasing Perry out of the offense, even though Joe still managed to rush for a respectable 602 yards in 1959. It became clear, however, that Hickey wanted to move Perry to another team. "Playing for Red Hickey was the worst time of my career," said Perry. "He was cleaning house with all us older guys."[20]

Perry played one final year for San Francisco, carrying the ball a mere 36 times for 95 yards in 1960. Prior to the 1961 season, he was traded to the Baltimore Colts in exchange for a third-round draft pick. Perry had a productive season for the Colts in 1961, rushing for 675 yards and catching a career-high 34 passes. He impressed his new teammates, including running back Lenny Moore, who called him "the best-conditioned athlete I ever saw. He was first-class in everything."[21]

By leading the club in rushing, he became the first running back in history to lead his team in that category in three different decades. As veteran *Baltimore Sun* columnist John Steadman noted, Perry was not yet ready to hang up his cleats. "He still had something left," said Steadman. "His heart was in San Francisco, but he had some great games for the Colts."[22]

Perry played one final year for Baltimore, but age was finally catching up with him. His average of 3.8 yards per carry was the second-lowest of his career. The Colts decided to use younger players and gave him his release in the summer of 1963.

Despite being thirty-six years old, Perry still had two offers to continue playing football. One came from the Pittsburgh Steelers, who wanted to reunite him with his old backfield mate, John Henry Johnson. Perry turned the offer down, a decision he later regretted. "The biggest mistake I made in football," he would say, "was not going to Pittsburgh. I wasn't ever out of shape, and I still could run."[23] Instead, Perry accepted an invitation from Vic Morabito to return to the 49ers. Jack Christiansen replaced Hickey as coach, but the team won just two games, the lowest total in franchise history. Perry decided to retire and finished his career with just 98 yards gained for the year.

Perry's stint as a special teams coach under Dick Nolan (right) was short-lived due to their rocky relationship.

A Proud Man

Following his retirement, Perry worked for a wine distributor in the San Francisco area. He returned to football in 1968 as a special teams coach with the 49ers. The job did not last long, however, as he and head coach Dick Nolan had difficulty getting along. He did some scouting for the club before leaving for good in 1974. He went back to selling wine before finally retiring to Arizona.

At the time of his retirement, Perry's 8,378 yards rushing was the top total in NFL history. He caught 241 passes in his career, scored 61 touchdowns, and played in three Pro Bowls. In 1969 he received his biggest thrill by being named to the Pro Football Hall of Fame. As he said, "There is no way anything could surpass that."[24]

Breaking into pro football at a time when black players were few and far between, Perry had to fight more than just an opponent in a different uniform. He had to battle for equal acceptance as a human being as well. The way in which he handled himself on and off the field helped blaze a path for other black players in the years that followed.

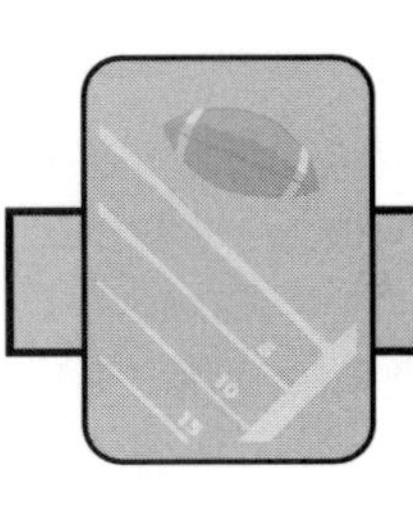

CHAPTER 3

Hugh McElhenny

Another member of the 49ers' Million Dollar Backfield, halfback Hugh McElhenny was quite possibly the greatest open-field runner the game has ever seen. Nicknamed "the King," he thrilled fans around the league with his slashing, darting runs, leaving opposing tacklers strewn in his wake. Veteran quarterback Y. A. Tittle called him "the greatest broken field runner I ever saw."[25] Anyone who saw him in his prime would most likely agree.

A Free Spirit

Hugh Edward McElhenny Jr. was born on New Year's Eve, December 31, 1928. He was raised with his younger sister in Los Angeles, within a few miles of his fellow Million Dollar Backfield teammate Joe Perry.

The Los Angeles of McElhenny's youth was more rural than the city of today, and Hugh enjoyed the freedom it afforded him. Hitching rides on freight trains was not an unusual event for the youngster. Neither was getting into fights and other kinds of trouble. At the 109th Street Grade School, where McElhenny attended classes, fights were a common occurrence. Hugh seemed to enjoy the confrontations, even more so when they disturbed his mother. He came home from one brawl with his white corduroy pants covered in mud. He later recalled, "When I got home, my mother told me if I ever came home like that again, she'd give me a whipping I'd never forget. That was a mistake, because then I began fighting all the time."[26]

McElhenny credits his running prowess to his defiant attitude. One day he stepped on a broken bottle and severed the tendons and nerves in his left foot. The doctors said the foot might not heal properly and might cause problems later on in life. Hugh was on crutches for a month, but he used his time in an unusual manner. Rather than attending to his schoolwork (he flunked fifth grade because of the injury), he used the crutches to help him develop athletically. "I could walk on crutches without using my feet," he related, "and I also played hopscotch and dodge ball on crutches."[27]

Some time later, after Hugh had fully recovered from his injury, his father became the owner of a company that rented pinball machines, jukeboxes, and other coin-operated machines. He was able

Halfback Hugh McElhenny (99) is considered one of the greatest open-field runners in NFL history.

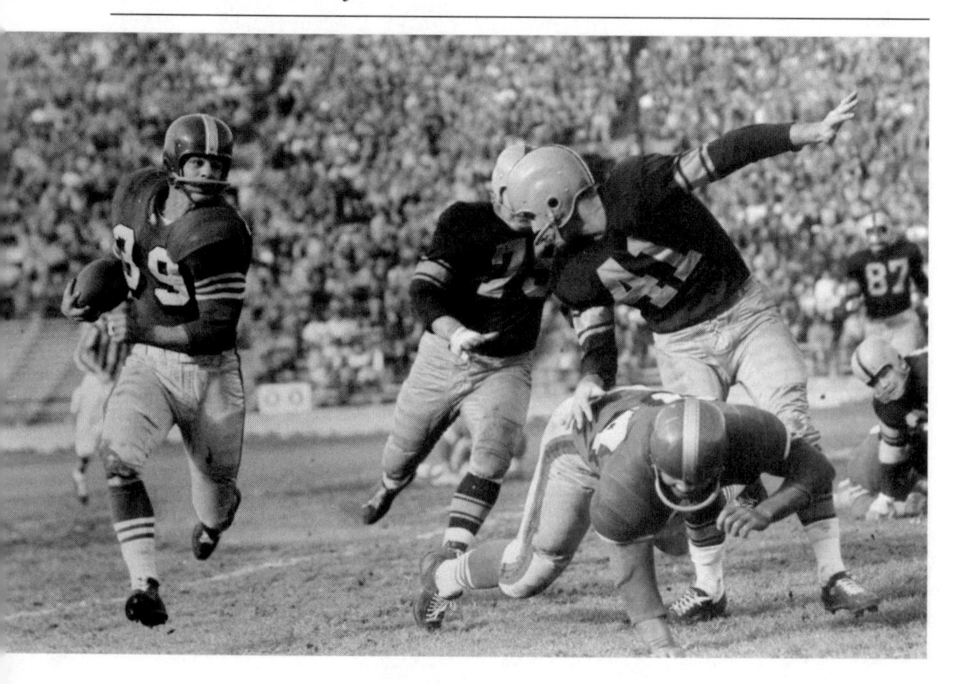

to move the family to a better neighborhood in the city. The change did young McElhenny a world of good. A metamorphosis began to take place as Hugh got involved in more wholesome activities, like joining the Boy Scouts and playing the trumpet.

Developing a Unique Style

McElhenny attended Bret Harte Junior High School, and it was there that he met his future wife, Peggy Ogston. As Peggy remembered, "He was a very considerate, very caring person. He knew his place and didn't take advantage. We got along, off and on. We were both stubborn. We broke up a lot."[28]

When they both moved on to George Washington High School, McElhenny joined the football team as a junior. He didn't see much action since he broke his collarbone in the very first game. By the time he was ready to return for his senior season of 1947, he had picked up some pointers from coach Bill Sloan that would help him develop his unique style of running. "First," related McElhenny,

> he said to drop my shoulder and lift up. This way, you don't take the brunt of the hit, and the tackler can't get to my legs. After being hit, I might bounce a few steps, but I'll keep on running. Second, he showed me how to use the straight-arm in order to get tacklers off balance. . . . I'd put a hand on a defender's head, not to jar him, but to push him. And his body would follow his head.[29]

Hugh developed another move on his own. He would drop what he called a "gimpy leg" in front of a tackler. When the would-be tackler made a move for him, McElhenny would lift his leg out of the tackler's grasp at the last possible moment and squirm free for more yardage.

Hugh's style of running was also influenced by his training in track and field, where he was a star hurdler. This helped him leap over tacklers and other defensive players. In fact, he trained arduously for the 1948 Olympics as a decathlete. He was forced to give it up, however, due to physical exhaustion. "At first, doctors thought it was the flu," he said, "but my body just broke down from months and months of training."[30] After graduating from high school, he never ran track again.

College Beckons

Hugh developed into an exciting runner, capable of turning a short gain into a touchdown with his elusiveness and speed. He was the best athlete in school and his future in sports looked bright. College scholarship offers came pouring his way, and he was tempted to enroll in the U.S. Naval Academy in Maryland. His fear of losing Peggy, however, kept him closer to home. He accepted a grant from the University of Southern California (USC) but lasted less than half a year at the school.

Around that time the young couple had another one of their periodic breakups. Hugh and a friend decided to get away from Los Angeles and see the country. They traveled halfway across the country, taking assorted jobs to earn money, then finally returned to California. As McElhenny later said, "What that trip taught me was that I didn't like hard labor, and I wanted to get an education."[31]

Hugh enrolled at Compton Junior College, where he became a sensation on the football team. He scored 23 touchdowns for the year, including one on a 105-yard punt return against the University of Mexico. His speed and agility made him a threat every time he touched the ball.

In the meantime, Hugh and Peggy had started seeing each other again. Hugh proposed, the couple got married, and they headed off to the University of Washington in Seattle, where Hugh continued his education. At Washington, McElhenny set many school and conference records during his three years on the football team. In his very first game as a sophomore, he returned a kickoff 96 yards for a touchdown. However, he hurt his foot later that same game and missed a good portion of the year. McElhenny bounced back in 1950 and led the Pacific Coast Conference with 14 touchdowns. In a game against Washington State, he rushed for a conference-record 296 yards on his way to collecting 1,107 for the year. Long runs and exciting kickoff returns became his trademark. Because of his exploits on the field, he became known as Hurryin' Hugh and Hurricane Hugh.

In 1951 the Huskies' All-America quarterback Don Heinrich suffered an injury and missed the entire season. McElhenny took on a bigger share of the offensive load, even kicking extra point attempts. He scored 125 points that year, ran for 906 yards, and caught 24 passes. In a game against USC, he returned a punt 100 yards for a touchdown to tie a National Collegiate Athletic Association (NCAA) mark. The kicker, former New York Giant Frank Gifford, remembered the play well. "I got the ball down in the corner," said Gifford. "The King took it there, right on the goal line. He started to weave down the sideline. All of a sudden, there was only one man, me, between him and the goal line. He left me flat on my face and ran it 100 yards."[32]

In his three seasons at Washington, Hugh set sixteen school records. He ended his college career by being named to the All-America team. In later years he would be honored as the Huskies' Football Player of the Century.

Next Stop, the Pros

Following the 1951 season, McElhenny appeared in several All-Star Games. San Francisco 49er quarterback Frankie Albert was impressed by what he saw of him in one such game and pleaded with San Francisco coach Buck Shaw to select McElhenny in the college draft. The 49ers did so with the ninth pick.

San Francisco 49ers quarterback Frankie Albert pleaded with coach Buck Shaw (center) to draft Hugh McElhenny.

With a wife to support, Hugh had not considered pro football as a long-term career. At most, he thought he would play "about three years, just enough to get a down payment on a house, a car, an investment."[33] He met with 49er owner Vic Morabito at a local restaurant to discuss his contract. McElhenny, on Albert's advice, asked for $30,000. As he later recalled, Morabito "told me they were thinking about something in the range of $5,000. . . . At that point he excused himself, got up and never came back. I even had to pick up the check."[34]

McElhenny eventually signed for $7,000. At the University of Washington, he had had a part-time job that required little actual work. He also received money from boosters, a common practice of the day that the NCAA did not crack down on until several years after his graduation. With this in mind, Albert introduced McElhenny to his new teammates by saying, "I'd like you to meet a man who took a cut in pay to become a professional."[35]

McElhenny's first game in a San Francisco uniform was an exhibition against the Chicago Cardinals. Although he had just joined the team and didn't even know his teammates, it didn't take him long to make an impression. McElhenny remembered:

> Frankie [Albert] had called a time out and asked Buck Shaw to put me in the game. Buck told him I didn't know the plays yet. . . . Frankie pretty much had his way with Buck, so Buck went along with him. In the huddle, Frankie drew a play on the ground and told everybody what to do. He threw me a pitchout and I ran 42 yards for a touchdown.[36]

Such explosive plays became commonplace occurrences at 49er contests. In the fourth game of the regular season, McElhenny took a punt on his own 6-yard line and ran it back 94 yards for a touchdown against the Chicago Bears. Those at the game were duly impressed. "McElhenny is the best running back I've seen in a long, long time," said former Bears quarterback and Heisman Trophy winner Johnny Lujack. Added legendary Chicago coach George Halas, "This guy is unfair. The commissioner should make him play with a different team every week."[37]

The Most-Feared Runner in the League

McElhenny had two other long runs that season—one of 89 yards and another of 82 yards—both against the Dallas Texans. Very quickly he became the most feared runner in the league. "He had star quality," said Albert. "Everyone appreciated Hugh, and he wore his acclaim well. He was cocky, but you liked his cockiness. He had a certain aura about him . . . when he grabbed the ball and got into the open field, everyone was on their feet. You knew that all hell was going to break loose."[38] Hugh finished his rookie year averaging an incredible 7 yards per carry in 1952. He scored 10 touchdowns and was named All-Pro.

The next year McElhenny received a raise in salary to $12,000. The 49ers finished with a 9-3 record, narrowly missing the playoffs. Hugh's total yardage dropped slightly, but he still provided more than his fair share of thrills. In one game against the Los Angeles Rams, he scored on what Rams coach Hampton Pool called "the most incredible run I've ever seen."[39]

In 1955 McElhenny added to his legend with another amazing run in a preseason game against the Pittsburgh Steelers. Hall of Fame quarterback Johnny Unitas, at the time trying to make the Steelers, described the action:

> I remember standing on the sideline, and watching McElhenny take a screen pass [a short pass to a back, in front of whom a wall of interference has been formed by the offensive linemen] from Tittle and running some fifty yards for a touchdown. But he must have run 150 yards to get the fifty. He crossed the field three times, stop, start, stop, start, and I don't think anyone touched him. I had heard of McElhenny before, but I just stood there amazed. It was one of the most thrilling things I saw Mac do.[40]

Unfortunately, the play ended with McElhenny hurting his foot after reaching the end zone. The injury would continue to bother him until it was corrected with an operation in 1956. McElhenny responded with one of the finest years of his pro career. He rushed for a career-high 916 yards and 8 touchdowns. He ran for 140 and 132 yards in two games against the Green Bay Packers, and in one game galloped 86 yards for a score.

A Change in Philosophy

The next year the 49er offense reflected a change in game philosophy. With R. C. Owens and the Alley-Oop play assuming a larger role, the passing game was stressed more than the run. As a result, McElhenny's rushing total dropped to 478 yards, but he caught a

R. C. Owens demonstrates his famous Alley-Oop catch, which changed the 49ers offensive approach to a passing game.

career-high 37 passes. One of those was the most important reception of his career.

Playing the Baltimore Colts in the eleventh game of the season, rookie quarterback John Brodie came in to replace the injured Y. A. Tittle with the 49ers trailing, 13–10. As Brodie recalled, "I asked Mac if he had anything. He said to throw the ball in the corner of the end zone, and he would catch it. I didn't know what he meant, but I threw it. He must have pushed Milt Davis ten feet to make the catch. Mac should have been thrown out of the game, but he got the touchdown."[41] The score gave the 49ers a 17–13 victory. The next week they defeated the Green Bay Packers to finish in a tie with the Detroit Lions for the Western Conference crown.

San Francisco lost the playoff game with Detroit for the right to go to the NFL Championship Game, but through no fault of McElhenny's. The King scored on a 47-yard pass play in the first quarter to give the 49ers a 14–0 lead. At the beginning of the third quarter, he broke loose on a 71-yard run to the Detroit 7-yard line. The Lions' defense held, however, and San Francisco had to settle for a field goal, giving them a 27–7 cushion. Unfortunately, the Lions bounced back to score 24 unanswered points, winning the game by a score of 31–27. McElhenny accounted for a solid 178 yards total offense. The defeat seemed to demoralize the 49ers, and it would be thirteen years before they made it back to the postseason.

Life After Thirty

McElhenny's production fell off drastically in 1959. New San Francisco coach Red Hickey handed the bulk of the rushing duties to J. D. Smith, and Smith responded with over 1,000 yards gained. McElhenny, although in good health, appeared to have lost some of his speed. He carried the ball only eighteen times all season.

The King saw slightly more action the next season, but it was obvious that Hickey wanted to phase out his older players. He traded McElhenny to the expansion Minnesota Vikings in the winter of 1961. Although he would have preferred to stay on the West Coast, McElhenny signed with the Vikings when they offered him a $25,000 contract.

Playing against his former teammates that year, Hugh showed that he still had a good bit left at age thirty-two. On one play from the 49ers' 32-yard line, he took the ball from quarterback Fran

Tarkenton and began to cut toward the sideline. He was pinned in but changed direction and began heading for the end zone. By the time he raced in for the score, he had escaped being tackled by seven San Francisco players who had gotten their hands on him. "It was the greatest run I ever saw," said Minnesota coach Norm Van Brocklin years later. "Whenever I think something's impossible, I put that film on the projector and watch it again." Even the 49ers couldn't believe what they had seen. "We started applauding," said 49er quarterback Brodie. "We didn't know what else to do."[42]

McElhenny had what he considered his best all-around season in 1961. He accumulated 1,067 all-purpose yards and scored 6 touchdowns. The Vikings voted him their most valuable player, as well as their team captain. He was also named to the Pro Bowl for the sixth time in his career.

After one more year in Minnesota, McElhenny was traded to the New York Giants. He had planned on retiring, but business problems made him reconsider. McElhenny had opened a grocery store—McElhenny Market—in 1959. He opened another one the following year, but his partners proved to be bad businessmen. McElhenny eventually had to declare bankruptcy. He was forced to continue playing football because he needed the money.

By 1963 McElhenny was a shell of his former self. Knee surgery had robbed him of much of his former speed and maneuverability. He was cut by the Giants after one season and signed with the Lions. He knew, however, that the end was near. "When the guards started to sweep," he said, "I couldn't catch them. My legs went dead."[43]

After leaving the active-player ranks, McElhenny worked for Burns Security in New York and an advertising firm on the West Coast. In the early 1970s, he was contacted by a group looking to bring pro football to Seattle. Because of McElhenny's reputation in the area, he was the perfect man to head the project. He was named executive vice president of a team that was to be called the Seattle Kings.

Unfortunately, things did not work out as planned. The Kings never materialized, but Seattle did get a professional football team when the Seahawks entered the league as an expansion club in 1976. McElhenny was proud of his role in bringing the pro game to the Northwest. "We didn't get credit for it," he said, "but we generated local enthusiasm for pro football in Seattle. We made it happen."[44] He left football following the 1964 season and is currently retired and living in Henderson, Nevada.

A Hall of Fame Career

In thirteen NFL seasons, McElhenny never played for a championship team and set few records. His all-around excellence, however, is illustrated by the fact that at his retirement he was one of only three players to accumulate more than 11,000 total yards on runs, catches, punt returns, and kickoff returns.

In 1970 McElhenny joined football's immortals in the Pro Football Hall of Fame in Canton, Ohio. "I never carried the ball that much," he said. "I never caught that many passes. I didn't get into

McElhenny stiff-arms a Bears defender, showing the mastery he exhibited in professional football.

the Hall of Fame by [setting] records, I guess it was the way I played the game."[45] His presenter that day, former 49er president Lou Spadia, agreed. "There are no statistics that can describe the beauty and artistry of McElhenny's running," he told the crowd. "He is the greatest runner of all times."[46]

The way he played the game thrilled everyone who saw him perform. He was a one-of-a-kind runner who was a threat to run for a touchdown any time he got his hands on the ball. Runners today may have more speed or more power, but none have perfected the art of the broken-field run as did McElhenny. He truly was—and shall always be—the King.

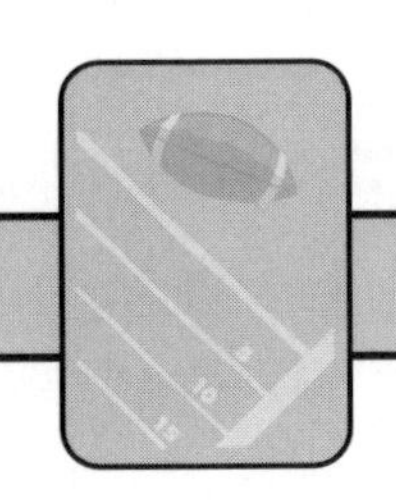

Chapter 4

Bill Walsh

Bill Walsh was the coach behind the dominant 49er team of the 1980s. The 49ers won three Super Bowl championships under his regime. As an innovator, he developed the short-pass-oriented West Coast Offense that quarterback Joe Montana ran to perfection. The former Stanford University head coach gained a reputation as a developer of quarterbacks, playing a key role in the schooling of Montana, Steve Young, and San Diego Chargers Hall of Famer Dan Fouts.

A Working-Class Family

William "Bill" Walsh was born in sunny Los Angeles, California, on November 30, 1931. His father was a laborer who worked in the city's railroad yards, brickyards, and auto repair shops. Money was hard to come by in the midst of the Great Depression, and prospects for the future weren't great. "There weren't any big plans for me," said Walsh. "We weren't a family that was destined for all that much."[47] Young Bill, however, had ambitions. "I wasn't going to let my life pass in a journeyman's role,"[48] he said.

Walsh took an interest in football at an early age. As a youngster, he would go to UCLA or USC games on Saturday afternoons and

Los Angeles Rams games, when possible, on Sundays. Like many other youngsters, he dreamed of someday playing in the NFL. Unfortunately, his talents did not take him that far.

As a running back at George Washington High School in Los Angeles, Walsh was good but nothing special. His dad moved the family to Oregon after Bill's sophomore year, then to San Francisco shortly after. Bill ran track and played football at Hayward High School, where the Fighting Farmers' head football coach Norm Sanders remembered him as "an intense player," although "I had no notion that he was even going to be a coach, let along a great one."[49]

Coach Bill Walsh developed the short pass–oriented West Coast Offense, leading the 49ers to three Super Bowl championships.

Walsh graduated from Hayward High School in 1949. He had hopes of attending either the University of California at Berkeley or Stanford University. Unfortunately, he had not applied himself in high school, and his grades were not up to the level required by the more acclaimed universities. Since he was not a standout athlete, he was not offered any football scholarships. With his parents unable to afford the tuition at the better-known schools, Bill decided to enroll at San Mateo Junior College.

At San Mateo, Walsh played quarterback on the football team. After two years he moved on to San Jose State University to get his degree. While there he played quarterback and both offensive and defensive end for coach Bob Bronzan's squad, all without distinguishing himself. "I never performed up to my athletic potential," remembered Walsh, "and that bothered the heck out of me years after I left. I was unhappy with myself and really determined to do well in whatever else I did."[50]

Despite Walsh's shortcomings as a player, Bronzan saw something he liked in the physical education major. Walsh's positive attitude and analytical approach convinced Bronzan that the young man had a future in coaching. He hired him in 1956 as a graduate assistant coach, giving Walsh a chance to get some coaching experience at the college level. Although Walsh remained in the position for only one year, Bronzan must have been impressed. He once predicted, "Bill Walsh will become the outstanding football coach in the United States."[51]

In 1957 Walsh secured the job of head football coach at Washington Union High School in San Francisco. The school did not have a good record in football, having won only once in the two years prior to Walsh's arrival. Within three years, however, Walsh turned the program completely around. He instituted a passing offense that was highly sophisticated for the high school level. At a time when most prep attacks were built around the running game, Walsh's teams had three or four receivers running patterns on every play. The opposing teams' defenses had difficulty adjusting to the variations. His players, however, had no such problems. By the time Walsh left after the 1959 season, Washington Union was the dominant team in its conference.

A Coach on the Rise

Walsh's coaching career was interrupted by a stint in the military service. After returning to San Jose State to earn his master's degree in physical education (his master's thesis was on "Stopping the Pro-Spread Offense"), Walsh accepted his first position at the college level. He was a recruiter and defensive coordinator under future Buffalo Bills coach Marv Levy at the University of California at Berkeley from 1960 through 1962. After that he joined John Ralston's staff at Stanford in a similar capacity.

Acutely aware of the importance of a good education, Walsh made sure his recruits had their priorities in order. "Walsh used the same recruiting pitch at both schools," wrote Tony Kornheiser in an article for *Inside Sports*, "emphasizing the academic reputation and telling students that by attending Cal [or Stanford] they could be 'better' than they were. On a number of levels, it was a class pitch."[52]

After four years at Stanford, Walsh began to attract the attention of the professionals. Al Davis, coach and president of the Oakland Raiders of the American Football League (AFL), hired him as the team's offensive backfield coach in 1966. The AFL had come into existence in 1960 as a challenger to the older National Football

Walsh accepted his first coaching position at the University of California at Berkeley under future Buffalo Bills coach Marv Levy (pictured).

League. In order to attract fans, teams in the new circuit featured a more wide-open, offensive style of play. Oakland used an offensive system adapted from the one used by the high-scoring San Diego Chargers. What Walsh considered "the most complicated offensive system the game has ever known,"[53] made a lasting impression on him.

Following his year with Oakland, the ambitious Walsh took a head coaching job with the semipro San Jose Apaches of the Continental Football League, another upstart league that hoped to win a share of the pro football dollar. By 1968, however, the franchise had folded and Walsh found himself back in the AFL, this time as offensive coordinator of the Cincinnati Bengals. "I was obviously overly ambitious to become a head coach," he admitted, "and things weren't happening fast enough to suit me."[54]

At Cincinnati Walsh worked under legendary coach Paul Brown, formerly of the Cleveland Browns. In eight seasons Walsh developed a reputation as an innovative offensive force, someone whose complex passing offense became the envy of coaches around the league. His system actually simplified the quarterback's job, removing the burden of having to figure out the defense. Three options were given on each pass play. The quarterback checked each one to see which player was open, then quickly threw the ball before the defense had a chance to react. Walsh was especially successful when it came to working with young quarterbacks, playing a substantial role in the development of Greg Cook, Virgil Carter, and Ken Anderson.

Unfortunately, the negatives at Cincinnati soon outweighed the positives. Walsh and his family missed being away from their home in California. Even more significant was his deteriorating relationship with Brown. Bill had been under the mistaken belief that he would be selected as Brown's successor when the head coach retired. When Brown finally stepped down on January 1, 1976, however, he named offensive line coach Bill Johnson to replace him. "That hurt both personally and professionally,"[55] admitted Walsh.

Walsh also discovered that the Houston Oilers had been interested in him as a possible head coach some years before. Brown had denied them the opportunity to speak to Walsh about the position, citing the fact that he was still under contract. Walsh resented the fact that he was never told about the offer. It was his belief that Brown did not want to take the chance of losing his highly valued assistant. "I was caught up in a syndrome where you become too valuable to someone and they can't afford to lose you," Walsh told Tony Kornheiser of *Inside Sports*. "I think I might have scared people off. I think my style may have been too penetrating. I wasn't your typical comfort-zone coach."[56]

Walsh moved on to the San Diego Chargers, where he became offensive coordinator under head coach Tommy Prothro. There he added to his résumé by installing his imaginative offensive system with Dan Fouts as quarterback. Fouts, who would be elected to the Pro Football Hall of Fame in 1993, credited Walsh with turning his career around.

After just one year at San Diego, Walsh accepted the head coaching job at Stanford University. Stanford's football program had been in decline, but he quickly turned it around. The Cardinals recorded sixteen wins in Walsh's two seasons in charge, and his starting quarterbacks—Guy Benjamin in 1977 and Steve Dils in 1978—led the NCAA in passing.

Walsh's performance at Stanford added to his reputation. "I think it became rather apparent that I was a very good football coach," he told Kornheiser. "Very few people become head coaches for the first time at forty-five. Major colleges wonder: Why weren't you a head coach before? Can you do the hard work? Stanford proved my vindication."[57]

Back to the Pros

During Walsh's tenure at Stanford, he was approached by both the Chicago Bears and the Los Angeles Rams about head coaching jobs. He turned the Bears down even though he was offered a $100,000 contract, more than twice his salary at Stanford. Walsh simply did not wish to leave his native California. "I don't even know why I talked to them, when I knew I wouldn't take the job," he later said. "Sometimes, you do things for your ego."[58]

In the case of the Rams, Walsh did not feel the position offered the security for which he was looking. He decided to stay at Stanford until a better opportunity came along. That opportunity was presented by the lowly San Francisco 49ers in 1979. The 49ers, who

In 1977 Bill Walsh took over the head coaching position for Stanford, quickly turning their program around.

finished with a league-worst 2-14 mark in 1978, gave the forty-seven-year-old Walsh a $160,000 contract. He also became the team's general manager, which gave him the final say in personnel decisions concerning the team.

Walsh began putting his intricate offensive system into place. The system called for a ball-control offense, but one that was dependent on short, high-percentage passes rather than runs, like the scheme Vince Lombardi had popularized in Green Bay. The key points in the system were explained by Lowell Cohn in a profile of Walsh in the *New York Times*:

> In other systems, the quarterback dropped back, tried to read the defense, then figured out which receiver was free against that formation. He had to do all this in about three seconds. . . . Walsh's quarterbacks do not have the burden of figuring out a defense. Walsh gives them three options to one-half of the field on every pass play. If the first receiver . . . is covered, the quarterback looks for the second, and so on. Someone is bound to be open, and the options are so quick that it is harder to sack or intercept a 49er quarterback than most others.[59]

In order to help his quarterbacks adjust to this new system, Walsh began "scripting" the first twenty or so plays of each game. This was designed to instill confidence in the offense and relieve the quarterback of the burden of making those decisions. The quarterback still, however, had the authority to change the play at the line of scrimmage if he saw a change in the defense.

Walsh's rookie season at the helm showed no difference in the standings. The 49ers finished with the same 2-14 record they had in 1978. A closer look, however, showed that progress had been made. The team's offense, led by quarterback Steve DeBerg, had improved significantly.

In 1980 the improved 49ers won six games, with Joe Montana replacing DeBerg as starting quarterback in midseason. The next season Walsh concentrated on improving his defense with astute draft picks. The results were impressive. The 49ers shocked the league by compiling an NFL-best 13-3 mark and going all the way to the Super Bowl. There they defeated the Cincinnati Bengals by a score of 26–21. The victory was made sweeter by the fact that Paul Brown was Cincinnati's general manager. Walsh showed his former boss that he was a more-than-capable head coach.

The Genius

Because of the transformation he had brought about with the 49ers, Walsh was nicknamed "the Genius" by the media. That reputation was enhanced in future years. His draft selections helped form the nucleus of the San Francisco team that would become the dominant team of the decade.

Following a disappointing 3-6 1982 season marred by a players' strike, injuries, and rumors of rampant drug abuse, Walsh seriously considered resigning. Owner Eddie DeBartolo convinced him to stay on but persuaded him to give up the job of general manager and add the less-demanding role of team president.

San Francisco bounced back to win the Western Division title in 1983. The following season the 49ers were favored to go all the way to the Super Bowl. Walsh had another excellent college draft, adding linebacker Todd Shell, tight end John Frank, guard Guy McIntyre, and linebacker/safety Jeff Fuller. The team didn't let its fans down, racing through their schedule and winning fifteen of sixteen regular-season games. As tackle Keith Fahnhorst described it, "We never felt the pressure of being a favorite because of Bill. From the very beginning of training camp, there was this calming feeling of complete confidence. Bill established this feeling. He just seemed, well, comfortable." Walsh agreed. "Yes, I was more comfortable," he said. "The reason was I had confidence in our staff and our players. We had grown together in 1983."[60]

The 49ers translated that feeling into wins over the New York Giants in the NFC Division Playoff Game (21–10) and the Chicago Bears in the NFC Championship Game (23–0). Behind the passing of Joe Montana and the running of Roger Craig, San Francisco routed the Miami Dolphins in Super Bowl XIX, 38–16, capping off a storybook season.

San Francisco 49er players raise Bill Walsh to their shoulders after defeating the Miami Dolphins in Super Bowl XIX.

The next year the 49ers failed to win their division and played the New York Giants in the wild-card playoff game. After New York came out on top with a 17–3 victory, Giants coach Bill Parcells sneeringly asked reporters, "What do you think of the West Coast offense now?"[61] From that point on, Walsh's system was forever identified by that name—even though it was developed in Cincinnati—oftentimes by coaches jealous of his success.

Following a first-round playoff loss to the Minnesota Vikings in 1987, Walsh was stripped of his presidency when the 49ers' ownership decided he was trying to do too much. They wanted him to focus solely on football and not on business projects such as the remodeling of Candlestick Park. The team bounced back to win its third Super Bowl the following season, but shortly after the victory, Walsh announced his retirement from the coaching lines. The pressures of coaching and a separation from his wife were affecting his emotions, as was his diminished role with the team. He moved into the front office, accepting the position of vice president of football operations.

Away from the Sidelines

In 1989 Walsh left the 49ers to take a job with the NBC television network as an analyst on American Football Conference (AFC) games. Although he got some good reviews, "He [is] no rambunctious John Madden," wrote *New York Newsday*'s Stan Isaacs, "nor is anybody else. Walsh does give indications, though, of being a likable, intelligent TV presence in the long run,"[62] he did not have a dynamic enough style to suit the network's executives and left after one season.

In 1992 he returned to Stanford as head coach. He remained three seasons but did not have the success he had in his first stint at the school. At this point in his life, Walsh was no longer interested in coaching and the responsibilities it entailed. In 1999 he accepted a general manager/consultant position with the 49ers, responsible for the evaluation of players. As he said, "I know I'll never coach again, so I had to decide what role I could fill. I decided I either wanted to come in at the very top, as the head of football operations, or at the bottom, as a consultant. . . . I realized that I no longer have the desire to put the time and effort into doing the job at the top that is necessary, so I thought I'd give this a try."[63] In May 2001 he stepped down as general manager and assumed the duties of vice president/consultant.

A Legendary Career

Bill Walsh was one of the most influential coaches in the history of the National Football League. He compiled a career record of 102-63-1, including a 10-4 mark in the playoffs. His 49er teams won six NFC Western Division titles and three Super Bowls. He was named the NFL Coach of the Year in 1981 and 1984 and Coach of the Decade for the 1980s.

One of the most influential coaches in NFL history, Bill Walsh led the 49ers to six NFC titles and three Super Bowls.

Walsh's major contribution to the game was as an innovator. His West Coast Offense has been copied by numerous coaches throughout the NFL. Former quarterback Steve Young said, "Bill was probably twenty years ahead of his time. He changed the game. Watch all the people using his stuff now."[64]

Part of Walsh's legacy is the number of distinguished coaches who either worked with him or learned under him. These include Pete Carroll, Bruce Coslet, Dennis Green, Jon Gruden, Paul Hackett, Mike Holmgren, Steve Mariucci, Ray Rhodes, George Seifert, Mike Shanahan, Dick Vermeil, Mike White, and Sam Wyche. As this network of disciples spreads his word, it ensures that his effect on the game will continue in the years to come.

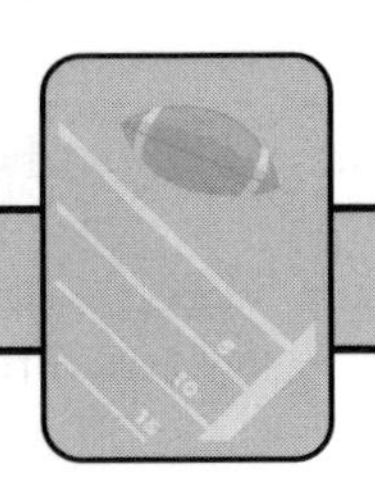

Chapter 5

Joe Montana

Joe Montana could not throw a football through a brick wall like Dan Marino. He could not scramble in order to avoid the grasp of enemy linemen like Fran Tarkenton. But Montana could win. As former teammate Randy Cross once said, "There have been, and will be, much better arms and legs and much better bodies on quarterbacks in the NFL, but if you have to win a game or score a touchdown or win a championship, the only guy to get is Joe Montana."[65]

Montana led the San Francisco 49ers to four Super Bowl victories over a span of nine years. His ability to remain calm no matter how stressful the situation was legendary. He never panicked and always seemed to come through when the team needed it most. Quite simply, Montana was the ultimate winner.

A Football Hotbed

Joseph Clifford Montana Jr. was born in New Eagle, Pennsylvania, on June 11, 1956. The town is located in western Pennsylvania, a region that has produced a bevy of National Football League quarterbacks over the years, including George Blanda, Jim Kelly, Johnny Lujack, Johnny Unitas, and Montana's personal hero, Joe Namath. The trait common to them all, according to Unitas, was their "no-nonsense, blue-collar background."[66]

Joe was the only child of Joe and Theresa Montana. His father was the manager of a finance company, and his mother a secretary with the same firm. He grew up in a middle-class neighborhood in Monongahela just south of Pittsburgh. Joe was encouraged in his love of sports by his father and developed into an all-around athlete. In Little League he pitched three perfect games and batted .500. When he got older, Joe excelled in baseball, basketball, and football at Ringgold High School.

Always calm under pressure, Joe Montana led the 49ers to four Super Bowl victories.

In high school football, Joe exhibited qualities that other quarterbacks sometimes took years to develop, such as the ability to look for secondary receivers when a play breaks down or the primary receiver is well covered. "Joe was born to be a quarterback," said his high school quarterback coach, Jeff Petrucci. "You saw it in the midget leagues, in high school—the electricity in the huddle when he was in there."[67]

In addition to his talents on the football field, Montana was proficient enough in basketball to be offered a scholarship to North Carolina State. After being named to the *Parade* All-America football team as a senior, however, he decided to stick with the gridiron and attend the University of Notre Dame, following in the footsteps of another western Pennsylvania quarterback, Terry Hanratty.

A Reputation for Comebacks

Joe's varsity debut at Notre Dame came in the third game of the 1975 season. At the time, he was the fifth-string quarterback. With his team trailing lightly regarded Northwestern University, 7–0, coach Dan Devine gave Joe his chance. Montana led the team to a 31–7 win, completing 6 of 11 passes for 80 yards and 1 touchdown.

The next week Joe performed more of his magic. Notre Dame fell behind the University of North Carolina by a score of 14–6. Montana entered the game and led the team to a tying touchdown. He then connected on an 80-yard pass to Ted Burgmeier for the winning score with just over a minute left to play. Montana led the Fighting Irish to one more come-from-behind victory that year. He brought the Irish back from a 30–10 deficit with only ten minutes to play to win 31–30 over the Air Force Academy.

A separated shoulder kept Joe out of action all of 1976. Partly because of the injury, he began the 1977 season third on the team's depth chart at quarterback. He awaited his turn to play and took advantage of it when it came. In the third game of the season, Notre Dame trailed Purdue, 24–14, when Montana entered the contest with two minutes left in the third quarter. He led the Fighting Irish to 17 points on 3 scoring drives over the last eleven minutes. His 9 completions in 14 attempts for 154 yards helped produce a 31–24 victory.

Coach Dan Devine was convinced of his ability and Montana took over the starting quarterback position. The team did not lose a game the rest of the season. When Notre Dame defeated the number one ranked University of Texas squad in the postseason Cotton Bowl, it earned itself the national championship and helped make Montana a national figure.

In the following year, Joe guided Notre Dame to a 9-3 record, with several come-from-behind wins. His greatest moment of all, however, came in the final game of his collegiate career. Notre Dame was playing the University of Houston on a chilly Dallas day in the 1979 Cotton Bowl. With a windchill factor of minus-ten degrees Fahrenheit, Notre Dame was trailing, 34–12. Montana de-

At Notre Dame, Joe Montana earned a reputation for comebacks.

veloped hypothermia from the cold and remained in the locker room after halftime, sipping chicken soup. He returned with eight minutes left in the game and led his team to 23 unanswered points. His touchdown pass to Kris Haines with no time remaining on the clock gave the Fighting Irish an amazing 35–34 victory. For his efforts, he was named the game's Most Valuable Offensive Player.

Joe ended his career at Notre Dame with 260 completions in 515 passes (.522) for 4,121 yards and 25 touchdowns. He graduated with a degree in marketing and looked forward to moving on to the National Football League.

A Lucky Pick

Despite Montana's success in college, professional teams were not convinced he could be a star since he did not possess a shotgun arm or an oversize body. However, the San Francisco 49ers eventually selected him in the third round. "What really impressed us," said former 49er quarterback coach Sam Wyche after having watched Montana work out for two days before the draft, "was that he could immediately put into practice any coaching suggestion. He would literally eat the words right out of your mouth. Call it what you will—intelligence, intangibles, charisma—that's what we saw in Joe."[68] Overall, he was the eighty-second player—and fourth quarterback—chosen that year.

Montana's arrival in San Francisco coincided with that of Bill Walsh, the former University of Stanford coach who took over as the 49ers' head coach in January. Walsh did not hand Montana the starting job when he joined the club. In fact, Joe sat on the bench for most of his rookie season, watching Steve DeBerg direct the team. The 49ers compiled a dismal 2-14 record, but with Walsh in charge, the offense was much improved from the previous year.

In 1980 Montana began the season alternating at quarterback with DeBerg. By the end of the year, he had earned the job outright. A high point of the season occurred on December 7 when the 49ers played the New Orleans Saints. Montana helped his team overcome a 35–7 Saints' halftime lead. San Francisco scored 4 unanswered touchdowns in the second half to tie the game, then won in overtime, 38–35. It was the first of 20 fourth-quarter comebacks Montana would engineer in his pro career. "That was really Joe's breakout game," said Walsh. "That gave him the confidence he could do the job."[69]

When the 1981 season came around, Montana was in command. Running Walsh's famous West Coast Offense (a pass-oriented system that placed an emphasis on quick, short passes), he led San Francisco to a 13-3 record while leading the league in pass-completion percentage for the second straight year. When the 49ers defeated the New York Giants in their first-round playoff contest, the stage was set for one of Joe's most memorable games.

The Catch

The NFC Championship Game was played at Candlestick Park against the Dallas Cowboys. The 49ers and Cowboys took turns scoring, and Dallas held a 27–21 lead with less than five minutes remaining in the game. The 49ers took over the ball on their own 10-yard line and Montana went to work. Mixing runs and passes to perfection, he drove San Francisco all the way to the Dallas 6-yard line with one minute left. The next play was arguably the most dramatic in 49ers history.

Montana throws the ball to Dwight Clark, who leaps high in the air to grab the touchdown in the 1981 NFC championship game. The play is now known as "The Catch."

Montana took the snap from center and circled to his right with two Dallas players in hot pursuit. He finally heaved the ball toward the back corner of the end zone, where tight end Dwight Clark leaped high to grab it for the game-winning touchdown. As Montana described it, "I thought the pass might have been a little high when I threw it, but I really didn't see it. I was knocked to the ground after I threw. I heard the roar of the crowd so I thought Dwight caught it. I didn't know what a great catch it was until I saw it later."[70] "The Catch," as it came to be known, put the 49ers in the Super Bowl for the first time in the team's history.

After the drama of the NFC Championship Game, Super Bowl XVI against the Cincinnati Bengals was almost anticlimactic. Montana scored 1 touchdown and passed for another as the 49ers built a 20–0 halftime lead. Joe completed 14 of 22 passes, ran for 18 yards, and was named the game's Most Valuable Player as the 49ers held on to win by a score of 26–21. The victory not only gave the 49ers the first world championship, but also their first world title in any major professional sport by a San Francisco team. Coach Walsh knew there was something special in the youngster. "Montana will be the great quarterback of the future," he said. "He is one of the coolest competitors of all time and he has just started."[71]

Another Memorable Matchup

Three years later Montana led the 49ers back to the Super Bowl. This time their opponent was the Miami Dolphins, who were led by their strong-armed quarterback Dan Marino. Marino had put together a memorable season in 1984, throwing for a record 48 touchdowns while guiding his team to a 14-2 record. Many expected him to be the difference in the game, despite the fact that the 49ers had set an NFL record for most wins in the regular season with 15. The lack of attention paid to the 49ers annoyed Montana. "You don't mind being overlooked that much," he said, "but sometimes it seemed [the media] forgot there were two teams in the game."[72]

He proved the media wrong. Super Bowl XIX was all about Joe Montana. He passed for 331 yards (24 for 35) and 3 touchdowns. He scored another touchdown himself on a 6-yard run. The final score was San Francisco 38, Miami 16. Montana was named the game's Most Valuable Player for the second time in his career. The Dolphins were effusive in their praise of him. "There's nobody else like him," said Miami's defensive coordinator, Chuck Studley. "The way he knows where he is, where his receivers are, that complete vision he has—it's unbelievable."[73]

The 49ers experienced a lull in the two seasons following their victory in Super Bowl XIX. The low spot came after the opening week of the 1986 season. Montana had to have surgery on his back, and it was suggested that his career might be over.

Joe surprised everyone, however, and returned to action seven weeks later.

Montana led the 49ers back to the playoffs, but San Francisco was trounced by the Giants, 49–3, in the wild-card game. Joe was knocked out in the second quarter and suffered a concussion. Because of the surgery and the concussion, many observers, including 49er head coach Bill Walsh, wondered how much longer Montana would be able to play. San Francisco obtained Steve Young in a trade with the Tampa Bay Buccaneers, expecting him to be their quarterback of the future. Montana, however, wasn't ready to call it quits. The trade marked the beginning of a heated rivalry between Montana and Young, both of whom wanted to be the starting quarterback.

The Rivalry

At the beginning of the 1987 season, the players' strike took some of the attention away from the quarterback competition. Although Montana was still the starter, his frequent injuries gave Young ample playing time.

Montana led San Francisco to a 13-2 record during the regular season. In the process he won the first passing title of his NFL career. He faltered, however, in the NFC Championship Game against the Minnesota Vikings and was replaced by Young early in the second half. It marked the first time Joe had ever been taken out of a game when he wasn't injured. The 49ers fought back valiantly, but the Vikings persevered and came out on top, 36–24.

The next season, when Bill Walsh was asked about his team's chances during a press conference, he conceded, "We may have a quarterback controversy."[74] Montana took the statement to mean that his days as a 49er might be numbered. He accepted the challenge and showed everyone he was not yet finished.

Although Montana continued to be the starter, his bad back and a bout with dysentery gave Young significant playing time as his backup. It was Montana at the controls, however, when the 49ers put together a five-game winning streak toward the end of the year that assured them of a place in the playoffs. There, Montana led San Francisco to surprisingly easy wins over both the Minnesota Vikings (34–9) and the Chicago Bears (28–3). With the 49ers on a roll, most observers made them a heavy favorite to defeat the Cincinnati Bengals in Super Bowl XXIII.

A Memorable Win

In the days leading up to the big game, the 49ers were distracted by rumors of Coach Walsh's possible retirement. When the game started, it appeared that the distractions had had an effect on the team's performance. Although San Francisco dominated play through most of the first three quarters, the Bengals held a 13–6 lead with one quarter left.

The 49ers tied the score on a Montana-to-Rice touchdown pass, but the Bengals regained the lead on a 46-yard field goal by Jim Breech. San Francisco returned the ensuing kickoff to the 20-yard line, but a penalty moved them back to their own 8-yard line with less than three-and-a-half minutes left in the game. It was enough time, however, for Joe Montana.

As the seconds ticked off the clock, Montana coolly connected on five consecutive passes to move the ball to the Bengals' 35-yard line. During one break in the action, he calmly looked toward the sidelines and said, "Hey, look, there's [comedian] John Candy!" Montana later explained, "[Tackle] Harrison Barton was always so up-tight, I just wanted to loosen him up. We had a time-out and Harris was just staring into space. I just wanted to get him to smile."[75]

The tension was broken and the 49ers were ready to get back to work. A penalty moved the ball back 10 yards but did not stop Montana, who connected on a 27-yard pass to Jerry Rice for another first down. After a short completion to Roger Craig, the 49ers called time-out with second-and-two from the Cincinnati 10-yard line.

Time was running out and the pressure was mounting. Montana, however, showed why he was called Joe Cool. On the very next play, he passed the ball to wide receiver John Taylor in the middle of the end zone for the winning touchdown and the 49ers' third Super Bowl victory of the decade. Montana later said that the play was the top Super Bowl thrill of his career.

The Seifert Years

As expected, shortly after the Super Bowl, Walsh announced his retirement. Defensive coordinator George Seifert was hired to replace him. Walsh's departure created a challenge for the team. His relationship with many of the players had deteriorated, and they wanted to show everyone they could win without him.

Luckily for Seifert, Montana would have the best season of his illustrious career in 1989. He led the 49ers to their fifth consecutive Western Division title with a 14-2 record. In so doing, he led the league in passing with an NFL single-season record quarterback rating of 112.4. In the third game of the year, he threw 4 touchdown passes in the last quarter to lead San Francisco to a come-from-behind 38–28 win over the Philadelphia Eagles. Eleven weeks later he completed 30 of 42 passes for 458 yards in a victory over the Los Angeles Rams.

Jumping for a high-five with teammate Guy McIntyre, Montana celebrates one of his 5 touchdown passes in Super Bowl XXIV.

As good as Montana was during the regular season, he was even better in the playoffs. In their first game, the 49ers trampled the Vikings, 41–3. The following week they breezed past the Rams, 30–3, with Joe completing an incredible 26 of 30 passes. Super Bowl XXIV against the Denver Broncos was even more one-sided. Montana completed 22 of 29 passes for 297 yards and a record 5 touchdowns. The 49ers made short work of the Broncos, winning by a 55–10 landslide. Montana won an unprecedented third Super Bowl MVP Award.

Having repeated as champions, the 49ers set a third straight Super Bowl championship as their goal for 1990. They came up just short, but through no fault of Montana's. San Francisco began the season with a team-record ten consecutive victories. In one game against Atlanta, Montana threw for a team-record 476 yards. In the second half of the year, however, his age and the wear and tear on his body began to show. The 49ers finished with a league-best mark of 14-2, but Montana's performance was beginning to decline.

The Beginning of the End

Montana's football future received a severe setback in the NFC Championship Game. Playing the New York Giants, the 49ers led, 13–12, with about three minutes left to play. Montana faded back to pass and was blindsided by New York defensive lineman Leonard Marshall. The ferocious hit resulted in a broken right hand, a bruised sternum, and a concussion for Montana, who had to be replaced by Young. The Giants went on to recover a Roger Craig fumble and score a field goal as time ran out, giving New York a 15–13 victory and sending them to the Super Bowl.

Injuries and three surgeries kept Montana out of action for almost two full seasons. He returned to play the second half of the last game of the 1992 season, but by then Young was Seifert's choice for starting quarterback. Some people in the San Francisco organization wanted Montana to be given the job back, but it was unrealistic to consider replacing the NFL's Most Valuable Player in 1992 (Young) with a thirty-seven-year-old man who had sat out two full seasons with injuries. The 49ers gave Montana the choice of staying with the team or trying to make a deal for himself with another club. Such a move was unprecedented when the player concerned was under contract.

Knowing he couldn't win out against the younger quarterback, Montana decided to go to the Kansas City Chiefs, who thought he could be the one to lead them to a championship. A deal was arranged, and Montana was sent to the Chiefs in exchange for a first-round draft pick. Montana was realistic about his situation. "If I go to Kansas City," he said, "I'll be the man. If I get injured, they'll pray for me to get well. If I get hurt here, I'll be pushed out the door."[76] Still, he was disappointed he could not finish out his career with San Francisco.

Walking Away from the Game

Montana played two seasons with the Chiefs, leading them on to the playoffs both years. In the 1993 AFC wild-card game, Kansas City trailed the Pittsburgh Steelers at halftime, 17–7. Montana brought the Chiefs back to tie the game at 24 points in a dramatic fourth-down touchdown pass to Fred Barnett. They went on to win in overtime to advance to the divisional playoff game against the Houston Oilers. Montana continued to perform his magic, with his 3 second-half touchdown passes helping Kansas City come back from a 10–0 halftime deficit to win by a score of 28–20.

Montana retired following the 1994 campaign. His ledger after sixteen NFL seasons showed 3,409 completions for 40,551 yards and 273 touchdowns. Since his retirement he has stayed out of the limelight, enjoying time with his family and friends. He has done some television work for NBC and continues to be on call for

Joe Montana was inducted into the Pro Football Hall of Fame in 2000.

speaking engagements. He has also gotten involved in auto racing as part owner of the Target Chip Ganassi Racing team.

His legacy cannot be measured in numbers alone. Montana was the player who led the 49ers to their first championship and helped keep them at, or near, the top of the league standings for more than a decade. "Without question," said Eddie DeBartolo. "He's the guy who started it all."[77] His coolness under fire was legendary, as was his ability to bring his team back to victory from the brink of defeat. Joe Montana, very simply, *was* the San Francisco 49ers. When he entered the Pro Football Hall of Fame on July 29, 2000, he brought with him the admiration of an entire city, a city that loved the man known as Joe Cool.

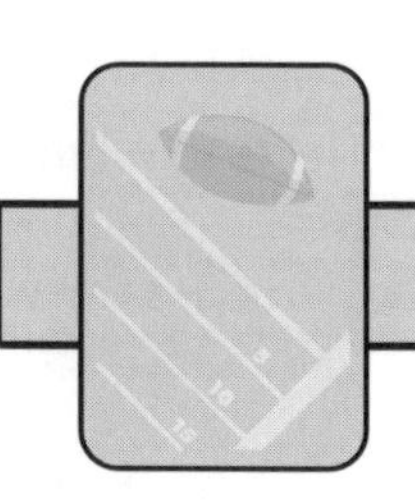

Chapter 6

Ronnie Lott

Perhaps Dallas Cowboys coach Tom Landry described Ronnie Lott as well as anyone. "He's devastating," said Landry. "He may dominate the secondary better than anyone I've seen."[78] Lott was a perennial Pro Bowl selection starting with his rookie season in 1981. Over the next decade and a half, his name became synonymous with an aggressive style and hard-hitting tackles, earning him a reputation as one of the greatest, most-feared defensive backs of all time.

Childhood in the Inner City

Ronald Mandel Lott came into the world on May 8, 1959. He was the oldest of three children born to Roy and Mary Lott of Albuquerque, New Mexico. Roy served in the U.S. Air Force. When Ronnie was five years old, his dad was assigned to Washington, D.C., where he chauffeured officers from Bolling Air Force Base to the Pentagon.

Growing up in Washington, Ronnie developed a love for all sports. He watched all that he could on television and spent the rest of his time playing outside with his friends. One of his favorite games was a one-on-one tackling game called "bull in the ring." "I've always loved the great hit," he said. "I like the contact of it. I grew up liking the velocity."[79]

Playing in the streets of the inner city toughened the youngster and helped him develop skills he would later apply to football. As Lott explained, "You learned how to compete. Either you were good or you didn't play."[80] Ronnie especially liked football. He enjoyed making believe he was his favorite player, wide receiver Charley Taylor of the Washington Redskins.

Defensive back Ronnie Lott was known for an aggressive style and hard-hitting tackles.

Ronnie's fearlessness was demonstrated at a young age. One Christmas he begged his parents for a new pair of sneakers. As his brother, Roy Jr., remembered, "To demonstrate how good the sneakers were, he jumped from our second-floor apartment window to the first-floor landing. That landing was only four feet square. He hit it perfectly and didn't even hurt himself. That really shocked me."[81]

On the Move

As a military man, Roy Lott occasionally was reassigned to other stations. When Ronnie was nine, the family moved west to San Bernardino, California, and shortly after to nearby Rialto. The moves were hard on Ronnie, who had to leave his old friends and try to make new ones. The one constant in his life was his family. "It was just the five of us," he remembered. "We made sure everybody shared, everybody gave. And we kept our focus humble."[82] The sharing even extended to sports. When Ronnie and his younger brother, Roy Jr., played Pop Warner football, his dad helped run the league, his mom handled the refreshments, and his sister, Suzie, was a cheerleader.

In Rialto Ronnie attended Eisenhower High School. He starred in baseball, basketball, and football, making the all-conference team in each sport three consecutive years. In football he played wide receiver, safety, and quarterback. He had 21 interceptions in his high school career and was named to the *Parade Magazine* High School All-America team in his senior year of 1976. Lott was courted by many colleges and eventually accepted a football scholarship to the University of Southern California.

As a freshman at USC, Ronnie was befriended by senior Dennis Thurman, a defensive back who would later play in the NFL with the Dallas Cowboys and Phoenix Cardinals. Lott credits Thurman with helping him mature as a football player. "Dennis was like a father to me in football," said Lott. "He began teaching me how to keep my head in the game at all times."[83]

Lott took Thurman's advice to heart. He was an All-American defensive back as a junior and finished second in the nation in interceptions as a senior. In addition to making All-America for a second time that year, Ronnie was also named USC's most valuable player and most inspirational player. He pushed himself as hard as he could, getting the most out of his ability. His performance served as an example for the rest of the team. The Trojans' defensive secondary that year was one of the greatest in college football history. All four starters—Dennis Smith, Jeff Fisher, Joey Browner, and Lott—had careers in the NFL after leaving school. Lott was the best of the group. He covered opposing receivers as if his life depended on it.

Lott graduated from USC with a degree in public administration in 1981. When the NFL draft was held that spring, the San Francisco 49ers selected him with their number one pick on the recommendation of defensive backfield coach George Seifert. It would be one of their best moves of the decade.

A Glorious Rookie Season

Nobody expected much of the 1981 San Francisco 49ers. The team was coming off a 6-10 record under second-year coach Bill Walsh after consecutive 2-14 marks in 1978 and 1979. Lott was positioned as the starting left cornerback on the first day of training camp. He teamed with Eric Wright, Dwight Hicks, and Carlton Williamson to form one of the best secondaries in the league.

The 49ers started the season out slowly, losing two of their first three games. They won their next seven contests, then dropped a 15–12 game to the Cleveland Browns. They would not lose another game all year. "The overall chemistry of that team was good," said Lott. "Everyone started to believe that we could win. There was a lot of fresh people that year who didn't know about the 49ers' past and didn't want to know."[84]

The turning point for the team was the sixth game of the year, against the Dallas Cowboys in Dallas. Lott intercepted two passes and ran one back 41 yards for a touchdown. The 49ers came out on top, defeating the Cowboys by a score of 45–14. The win proved to the young players they could successfully compete against the better teams in the league. "That was a big game for me," remembered Lott, "because I had a lot of admiration for some people on the Dallas team. . . . I was able to pick off a couple of passes and made some tackles. When you play against people you admire, you want to play good against them."[85]

With Joe Montana guiding the team at quarterback, the 49ers compiled a 13-3 record in the regular season. They continued their

Ronnie Lott is carried off the field by ecstatic fans after winning Super Bowl XVI.

surprising run through the playoffs, first defeating the New York Giants, 38–24, in the NFC Division Playoff Game. The next week they again played the powerful Cowboys in the NFC Championship Game. In that contest Lott intercepted a pass intended for Drew Pearson but was called for interference, giving the Cowboys the ball on the San Francisco 12-yard line. Replays, however, showed that if interference was called, it should have gone against the offense. The Cowboys scored, giving them a 17–14 lead at halftime. San Francisco rebounded in the second half and came away victorious as Montana completed "the Catch" to Dwight Clark with time running out. The victory put the 49ers in Super Bowl XVI, where they easily handled the Cincinnati Bengals. Lott helped the defense hold the Bengals scoreless in the first half as San Francisco bolted to a 20–0 lead. The 49ers held on in the second half, winning by a score of 26–21 to take their first NFL title.

Lott recorded 7 interceptions on the year—returning 3 for touchdowns—and was one of six San Francisco players named to the Pro Bowl. He also earned All-Pro honors and finished second in the voting for Rookie of the Year. His all-out style of play earned him recognition and respect around the league. Opposing receivers knew they would be hit hard if they caught the ball anywhere in Lott's vicinity. As former teammate Fisher said, "We knew he would be a great safety, but we never knew he could play the corner. What [it] told you was whether he played cornerback or safety, he was going to come up and hit you."[86]

After winning a championship ring as a rookie, Lott's sophomore year in the league left something to be desired. The players' strike caused the season to be cut short, and an injury kept him out of action for seven weeks. In spite of his limited playing time, Lott still made the Pro Bowl as the 49ers won just three of their nine games.

A Change in Outlook

Until 1982 Lott's aggressive demeanor on the field was reflected in his attitude toward the fans. A combination of factors caused him to change his outlook, as he explained in an interview. "I was being selfish," he said. "I wasn't giving that year. . . . That year was full of misfortune. There was the strike. I was in a car wreck. Our team wasn't winning. That's when I decided that the more I give in life, the more I get in life."[87] The change in attitude was readily apparent. It would not be long before Lott became known as one of the game's real gentlemen. "It's easy to help others," he told *Sports Illustrated*'s Jill Lieber years later, "to give them some hope, some belief that they can make it. You've got to share yourself. You can't forget where you came from and that you should help people. The rewards you get from that are better than any others."[88]

The 49ers returned to form in 1983, winning the NFC's Western Division crown and defeating the Lions in the first round of the playoffs. The team lost to the Washington Redskins in the NFC Championship Game, however, in part because of a questionable holding call against Lott.

The succeeding seasons found Lott establishing a standard of excellence that was difficult to match. He split his time between the cornerback and free safety positions in 1984 as San Francisco fielded one of the league's greatest teams ever. The 49ers' only loss was to the Pittsburgh Steelers, 20–17, in the seventh game of the season. They rolled through the playoffs and met the Miami Dolphins in Super Bowl XIX.

Before the big game, Miami receiver Mark Clayton tried to downplay Lott's influence on the game. "All I'm hearing about," he said, "is Ronnie Lott, Ronnie Lott. He's not on a pedestal, you know.

A player who liked to let his actions speak for him, Lott smashes into Mark Clayton in the end zone.

He takes chances, and he can be beat." Lott preferred to let his actions speak. "We certainly are going to make sure they know we are there,"[89] he said. During the game Lott broke up three Dan Marino passes to Clayton, including one in the end zone. He helped hold Marino to a single touchdown pass in the game. The Miami quarterback had thrown for an NFL-record 48 that season, an average of 3 per game. The 49ers won the game by a score of 38–16.

Changing Positions, Changing Roles

The years that followed saw Lott solidify his standing as one of the great defensive backs in the game. However, by 1986 he was playing the free safety position full-time. He adapted well to the new spot and led the NFL with 10 interceptions.

Two years later Lott became even more of a team leader than he had been in the past. "I felt compelled to take over more than usual," he explained to Frank Cooney of *The Sporting News*, "because . . . I realized this was a team that could go in either direction. Instead of motivating myself, I was pushing other people. I found myself exhausted mentally trying to keep everybody levelheaded."[90]

Nowhere was his influence seen more than in Super Bowl XXIII against the Cincinnati Bengals following that 1988 season. Bengals' running back Ickey Woods had rushed for more than 1,000 yards that year. Early in the game, Lott delivered a fierce hit that seemed to unnerve the Cincinnati rookie. Until that point, said San Francisco defensive coordinator George Seifert, "Ickey Woods was playing at a different tempo than the rest of us. Ronnie Lott had a direct impact on us winning that ball game."[91]

San Francisco head coach Bill Walsh retired following the Super Bowl win, and Seifert was named to replace him. Along with Walsh's well-deserved reputation came the feeling shared by many that he alone was responsible for the team's success. Many of the players, including Lott, resented this and took it upon themselves to make 1989 the "We'll show Walsh" year. The team took up the challenge and dominated play all year. In Super Bowl XXIV, they routed the Denver Broncos, 55–10, to win their second consecutive title. Lott helped the 49er secondary hold Denver and John Elway to just 103 yards passing, a meager total for one of the league's top passing attacks.

A Parting of the Ways

Injuries were starting to take a toll on the hard-hitting Lott. The thirty-one-year-old missed five games during the 1990 season as the 49ers came up short in their bid for an unprecedented third straight Super Bowl win. Team officials began to wonder how much longer he could continue to punish his body.

At that point in time, in an attempt to avoid true free agency for players, the NFL had instituted what was known as Plan B. Under this plan, a team could protect thirty-seven of its players while the others became free agents, able to sign with whichever team they wished. High-salaried veterans were often left unprotected, with the assumption being that other teams would be hesitant to take on these players.

As part of this strategy, the 49ers did not protect Lott that year, even though they wanted to re-sign him. When Ronnie found out about the situation, his pride was irreparably damaged. He chose to leave the 49ers and signed a two-year contract with the Los Angeles Raiders. The team lost one of its biggest enforcers. Lott's first season with the Raiders saw him lead the league in interceptions for the second time in his career. He downplayed the idea that he had extra motivation to show the 49ers they were wrong to let him go. "If that's the standard I use to live my life," he said, "it's pretty shallow. My standards are a bit higher than that."[92]

Lott played one more year with Los Angeles, then signed as an unrestricted free agent with the New York Jets in March 1993. New York was thrilled to get the thirty-four-year-old veteran. "You don't find a Ronnie Lott every day," explained Jets coach Bruce Coslet. "He doesn't have to change for us. He fits perfectly."[93]

The Jets fell short of the playoffs in 1993, but Lott's presence and leadership made him an important part of the team. Always willing to put the team's needs ahead of his own, he agreed to take a $325,000 pay cut for 1994 in order to free up money for the team to sign other players. Lott's selfless attitude did not go unnoticed by Jets general manager Dick Steinberg. "In the short period of time that Ronnie Lott has been with the Jets," he said, "his contributions both on and off the field have been tremendously important to our organization. Today's move is just another example of his unselfishness and desire to help the team win any way possible."[94]

On to Canton

Ronnie Lott signed up again with San Francisco following the 1994 season so that he could retire as a 49er. He finished with 63 career interceptions to his credit, fifth on the NFL's all-time list. His total of 9 in postseason play is unsurpassed. Lott also holds the distinction of being the only player in league history to be named All-Pro at cornerback, strong safety, and free safety.

Since his retirement, Lott has been involved in a variety of undertakings. He is a cofounder and general partner of Champion Ventures, a venture capital investment firm. He is a spokesman for several national companies, including Nike, Coors, and DIRECTV. He has maintained contact with football with a weekly football show for FOX Sports. Lott also spends time involved in charitable work, much of it through his nonprofit organization, All Stars Helping Kids. Plus he hosts an annual celebrity golf tournament to raise funds for disadvantaged children in the San Francisco Bay area.

One of the most intimidating defenders of all time, Lott's passion and intensity landed him in the Pro Football Hall of Fame.

Lott was arguably the most intimidating defensive back of all time. His passion and intensity combined to make opposing teams focus their attention on him. There was no player who ever gave more of himself every minute he was on the field. An often-retold story recounts how he caught his finger in an opponent's face mask in 1985. Rather than have surgery and miss time while the finger healed, he had the tip of the finger amputated.

Respect provided the basis for Lott's motivation on the field. As fellow Hall of Fame inductee Joe Montana said when the two best friends were inducted together into the Pro Football Hall of Fame in Canton, Ohio, in 2000, "On the field and off the field, Ronnie is what a teammate is supposed to be. Ronnie speaks and Ronnie delivers. He could talk the talk and walk the walk."[95]

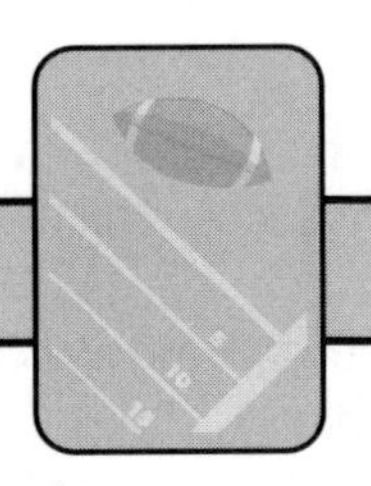

CHAPTER 7

Jerry Rice

Jerry Rice holds almost every NFL career receiving record in both the regular season and the postseason. Having been dominant for such a long period of time, he unquestionably is the greatest wide receiver the league has ever seen. Former 49er head coach and general manager Bill Walsh goes even further. "Irrespective of position," says Walsh, "Jerry could be the greatest football player of all time."[96]

Rice owes his success to a legendary work ethic. "He has a serious competitive drive and a desire to excel every time he steps on the field," said former All-Pro wide receiver Paul Warfield. "Combine that with his ability—great hands, outstanding body control, great instincts—and his intellect for the game, you have something truly special."[97]

A Rural Beginning

Jerome Lee Rice was born on a farm near the tiny town of Crawford, Mississippi (population 500), on October 13, 1962. His parents, Joe Nathan and Eddie B., had eight children. Joe earned a living as a brick mason, but with ten mouths to feed, the family struggled to get by.

As a child, Jerry was quiet and shy. He spent much of his time at home, occasionally walking or running to friends' houses several miles away. Although he had a happy childhood, he once told an interviewer, "When you live in Crawford, all you want to do is get out."[98]

Like most youngsters, Jerry liked physical activity. He loved running through the fields and chasing his neighbors' horses. He also enjoyed working with his hands and found he had a gift for fixing things. His goal was to open a shop someday where he would fix broken toys and appliances, or else become a mechanic and work with cars.

One thing Jerry knew he did not want to be was a bricklayer. During the summers he and his brothers used to help their father lay brick. The long, hard hours in the sweltering heat were rough on the youngster but helped him get into good physical shape. Pushing wheelbarrows loaded with bricks built up his endurance and upper-body strength. "It taught me the meaning of hard work,"[99] he later said.

Indirectly, the work also helped him improve his football skills. As he explained to Tom Fitzgerald of *The Sporting News*, "I would be standing on this tall scaffold and [my brothers] would toss the bricks up to me. I was catching bricks all day. One of my brothers would stack four bricks on top of each other and toss them up. They might go this way and that, and I would catch all four. I did it so many times, it was just a reaction."[100]

Without regard to position, Jerry Rice could be the greatest football player of all time.

A High School Standout

Jerry attended B. L. Moor High School, where he was an outstanding athlete. He averaged 30 points per game for the basketball team and high-jumped six feet eight inches as a member of the track-and-field team. He never forgot his responsibilities at home, however. "If he ran track on a Saturday," said his mother, "he'd be sure to do all the yard work early on a Friday. And if the track meet happened to be on a Friday, why, he'd do all his yard work on Thursday."[101]

Rice did not try out for football, however, until "convinced" to do so by the school's assistant principal in his sophomore year. As Jerry explained, "I was . . . playing hooky from classes when the [assistant] principal spotted me in the halls. When I heard him call my name, I took off. All he saw was the back of my red jacket."[102] When Rice was finally caught, the assistant principal told him that the football team could use someone with his speed. Given a choice between trying out and being punished, Rice chose football.

Jerry made the team, but his mother was not in favor of him playing. "I didn't love it," she said, "but the more I fought it, the more determined he was, so I gave it up. You just never know what God has in the storehouse for you."[103]

Right from the beginning, Jerry showed he had the makings of a star. He played several positions, including running back, tight end, and cornerback, but made his biggest impact as a wide receiver. Moor compiled a 17-2 record in Rice's final two seasons, but few other statistics were kept since the school was so small.

Similarly, because of the school's size, few college coaches were aware of Rice's record. He wanted to attend nearby Mississippi State University, but no one from the school ever saw him play. He finally received a scholarship offer from Mississippi Valley State University, a school in the smaller Division I-AA classification.

It did not take Delta Devils head coach Archie Cooley long to realize what he had in the young receiver. As noted by Ralph Wiley of *Sports Illustrated*, Cooley was soon "devising all manner of bizarre formations designed to spring Rice loose."[104] The coach's plan worked to perfection. Rice thrived at Mississippi Valley, setting eighteen Division I-AA records in his four seasons at the school. In his senior year, he caught an incredible 24 passes in one game and scored 28 touchdowns in the season.

Despite playing for such a small school, Rice still managed to attract the attention of scouts from NFL teams. Because of the lower level of competition at the I-AA school, more than one person had doubts as to Rice's ability to handle the rigors of the pro game. It would not take long, however, for Jerry to prove the doubters wrong.

Starring in the Pros

One of those who disagreed with the skeptics was San Francisco head coach and team president Bill Walsh. He selected Rice with the 49ers' first-round pick—and the sixteenth overall—in the 1985 college draft. In Rice, Walsh saw the deep threat the 49ers lacked: a player who could break open a game with one play and make their offense even more unstoppable.

Although Rice was the starting wide receiver as a rookie, he struggled through his first season. The structure of the pro game was a big change after playing in college. "At Mississippi Valley," he said, "I had the option of running any route I wanted, and I became accustomed to that freedom." In the professional game, he found himself "spending too much time . . . thinking about what I had to do instead of concentrating on the ball." Added quarterback Joe Montana, "Something that's typically rookie, he tried running with the ball before he caught it."[105]

Another factor affecting his performance was his newfound wealth. Never having had any money, it was only natural that he would start shopping for things he couldn't afford in the past. "It was a big change," said Rice. "I never had access to so much money, so that was a distraction."[106] The result was numerous dropped passes and the beginnings of self-doubt. Despite these problems, Rice still managed to catch 49 balls for 927 yards and was named the National Football Conference Rookie of the Year.

The turning point for Rice came in the fourteenth game of the year. The 49ers played the Los Angeles Rams, and Jerry caught 10 passes for a San Francisco single-game record 241 yards. The dropped passes stopped and his self-confidence began to return. The real Jerry Rice was about to step forward.

Catching the ball with one hand, Rice demonstrates his ability to break open a game with one play.

Silencing the Critics

During the off-season, Rice worked hard to learn all the complexities of the 49ers' playbook. He was determined to make up for the disappointments of his rookie year. Despite the fact that regular quarterback Montana was hurt for a good part of the year, Rice's performance improved significantly in 1986. In one game against the Indianapolis Colts, he caught 6 passes for 172 yards and 3 touchdowns. Rice remembered the game well. "There was something about that game that put me on the right track," he would later say. "I felt like I could do anything I wanted."[107]

For the year Rice had 86 receptions, second in the league to Todd Christensen of the Raiders. His speed and sure-handedness helped him record 1,570 receiving yards, the third-highest total in league history. In two short years, he had become one of the most-feared wide receivers in the game. In recognition of his performance, *Sports Illustrated* voted him the NFL Player of the Year.

Unfortunately, Rice's season ended on a negative note. With no score in the first quarter of the NFC Division Playoff Game against the New York Giants, Rice caught a pass from Montana and headed for the end zone. Without being touched, however, he fumbled the ball and the Giants recovered it. New York went on to crush the 49ers, 49–3, so the play had little effect on the outcome. Nevertheless, as Rice confessed, "The play will always linger in the back of my mind."[108]

The following year Rice firmly established his position as one of the league's best receivers in the strike-shortened 1987 season. Along with 65 receptions, he broke a pair of league marks. He caught a total of 22 touchdown passes, eclipsing the old record of 18 set by Mark Clayton of the Miami Dolphins in 1984. By the end of the year, he was working on a streak of 13 straight games with touchdown catches, surpassing the old mark of 11 held jointly by Elroy "Crazy Legs" Hirsch and Buddy Dial. For his heroics, Rice was named the NFL's Most Valuable Player.

In the playoffs he met with disappointment once again. After finishing the year with a league-best 13-2 mark in the regular season, the 49ers were considered the favorites to win the Super Bowl. In the first round, the Vikings pulled off an upset, defeating San Francisco, 36–24. Rice caught only 3 catches for just 28 yards. It was a disappointing end to what had been a spectacular season. Rice's dream of winning a Super Bowl ring had to wait another year.

Super Bowl Heroics

An ankle injury hampered Rice for much of the 1988 season. Even at less than 100 percent, however, he was still impressive. He worked extra hard to compensate for his loss of speed and caught 64 passes for the year, averaging better than 20 yards per reception.

Nine of his catches went for touchdowns, including a 96-yarder against the San Diego Chargers to set a 49er record.

By playoff time Rice was at full strength. In the NFC title game against the Chicago Bears, he caught 5 balls for 133 yards and a pair of touchdowns. His first score came late in the first quarter on a 61-yard pass from Montana, giving San Francisco a 7–0 lead. The 49ers were never headed, downing the Bears, 28–3. Jerry and his teammates were going to the Super Bowl to play the AFC champion Cincinnati Bengals for the title.

In the week before the big game, Rice twisted his ankle in practice. Despite the injury, he was, as Bengals' coach Sam Wyche later said, "the difference in the game."[109] With San Francisco trailing by 3 points with 34 seconds left, the 49ers had the ball on their own 8-yard line. Quarterback Montana led them 92 yards for the winning touchdown. Three of the plays on that last drive were passes to Rice, including a 27-yarder that set up the final score. Rice considered that final drive the favorite moment of his pro career. "Being able to come in in a crucial situation like that and being able to function," he said, "knowing that everything is on the line: a dropped ball, a fumble, and the game is over. That's the ultimate. I think that drive will no doubt be a part of me forever."[110]

Rice caught 11 passes in the 20–16 49ers' win for a Super Bowl–record 215 yards. He was named the game's Most Valuable Player, outdistancing Montana by a vote of 11–1. Accolades came his way from his teammates and coaches. Free safety Ronnie Lott stated, "I've said it all along that Jerry Rice is the best wide receiver ever to play this game."[111]

Two days after the game, Rice made some comments about the MVP Award that brought criticism his way. People felt he had implied that racism was a factor in what he perceived as a lack of recognition and scarcity of endorsements when a black player received an award such as the MVP. "If it were Joe Montana," he said, "it would be headlines all over."[112] Rice denied he was suggesting racism, but rather bemoaning what he saw as a lack of respect for his accomplishments.

However, there was no doubt that he had the respect of his teammates. "He was playing on guts," said Roger Craig. "He played hurt all year. But if there is a war breaking out, you can count on him being ready for it."[113]

Rice was certainly ready for 1989. Having won a Super Bowl, the 49ers' next goal was to repeat as champions. Rice had another marvelous season, leading the league with 1,483 yards receiving and 17 touchdown catches. The 49ers ran over the opposition, winning fourteen games and losing only two.

Rice kisses the Super Bowl XXIII trophy. He also received the MVP award for that game.

San Francisco's performance in the playoffs was even more dominating. In the opening round, they defeated the Minnesota Vikings, 41–13. Rice scored twice, including once on a 72-yard pass from Montana. The Los Angeles Rams provided little resistance in the NFC Championship Game. They lost to the 49ers, 30–3, as Rice caught 6 more passes.

In Super Bowl XXIV, the Denver Broncos didn't stand a chance. Montana threw five touchdown passes, including a Super Bowl–record 3 to Rice. All told, Rice caught 7 passes for 148 yards. The 49ers trampled the Broncos, 55–10, in the most one-sided Super Bowl ever played.

The Record Setter

The 49ers missed going to a third straight Super Bowl in 1990, but the season was still a memorable one for Rice. Despite his status as one of the top players in the league, he continued to work as hard as ever to maintain that standing. The results were impressive. In October he caught 13 passes for 225 yards and 5 touchdowns against the Atlanta Falcons. The touchdowns tied an NFL single-game record, one of many he would set over the next couple of years. For the season he led the league with 100 catches, making him just the third player in league history to reach the century mark. He also led in receiving yardage and was named the Player of the Year by *Sports Illustrated*. By now Rice's performance had made him the standard against whom other players were compared. "We're all measured by how we do against Rice," said New Orleans Saints cornerback Robert Massey. "I remember the first time an NFL scout talked to me right before the draft. The only thing he asked me was if I thought I could cover Jerry Rice."[114]

As Massey would find out, few cornerbacks could cover Rice. Two years later he caught the 101st touchdown pass of his career to break the record formerly held by Steve Largent. In November 1993 he established a *Monday Night Football* mark with his eighteenth career touchdown reception on the long-running weekly series of games. The following September, his three scores in the opening game of the season against the Los Angeles Raiders included the 127th of his career to move him past the immortal Jim Brown into first place on the all-time touchdown list. He finished that season with a team record 112 catches for 1,499 yards and 13 touchdowns. To top off the year, he scored 3 touchdowns in Super Bowl XXIX, as the 49ers defeated the Chargers, 49–26.

In 1995, at the age of thirty-three, Rice had perhaps the best season of his career. He caught a career-high 122 passes, one shy of Herman Moore's NFL record, and set a single-season mark for receiving yards with 1,848. By the end of the year, he was the league's all-time leader in both categories, with 942 receptions and 15,123 yards gained.

The following year Rice led the league with 108 catches, making him the first player in history to catch 100 passes in a season four times. He also became the first player with 1,000 career receptions and 16,000 receiving yards. By now he was San Francisco's all-time leading scorer, having moved past Ray Wersching with 982 points. In 1997 he added to his total, making him the first nonkicker in history to reach 1,000 points.

The End of an Era

Rice's run at the record books was slowed in the opening game of the 1997 season. He suffered torn ligaments in his left knee when he was thrown to the ground by Tampa Bay Buccaneer defensive tackle Warren Sapp. Shortly after his return three months later, he had his kneecap broken in a game against the Broncos and was out the rest of the year. The thirteen games he sat out were the first ones he missed due to injury in his entire career.

Rice bounced back in 1998 to finish with a team-leading 82 catches for 1,157 yards and his twelfth career Pro Bowl selection. Terrell Owens and J. J. Stokes, however, had taken over larger shares of the receiving duties. With quarterback Steve Young distributing the ball, each of the two youngsters recorded over 60 catches. It was obvious that the thirty-six-year-old Rice was no longer the team's future.

When Young went down with a season-ending injury in the third week of the 1999 campaign, it signaled the beginning of the end for an NFL dynasty. The 49ers finished the year with a 4-12 record, snapping the streak of sixteen consecutive winning seasons. With Jeff Garcia seeing the bulk of the playing time at quarterback, Rice caught 67 passes to lead the team once again.

However, prior to the start of the 2000 season, Rice signed a new five-year, $31.3 million contract extension that both he and the

49ers agreed would allow him to finish his career with the club. Unfortunately, such was not to be the case. He accepted a diminishing role on the team, happy to let younger players like Owens and Stokes play larger roles. "I think I'm having a better time now," he said, "because over the years, it's like the focus, it was always on me. So I had to perform on every given down, on every Sunday. Now, things have changed a lot and I can kick back and watch the young guys go to work."[115]

Rice still caught 75 passes, second to Owens's 97. In the world of modern-day pro football, however, catching passes is sometimes not enough. The 49ers were reluctant to commit to Rice's $2.5 million salary for 2001. By the middle of the season, it became obvious that he would not be back with the 49ers. San Francisco offered him a $1 million bonus to retire, but Rice declined.

On June 4, 2001, the 49ers announced that Rice had been given his release. The next day the NFL's all-time leading receiver and touchdown scorer signed a contract with the Oakland Raiders. The

Jerry Rice celebrates as he scores his first of 3 touchdowns in Super Bowl XXIX.

Rice era in San Francisco had officially come to an end. The final accounting for his sixteen years with the 49ers shows 1,281 receptions, 17,612 receiving yards, 187 touchdowns, 14 NFL records, 12 trips to the Pro Bowl, 10 selections to the All-Pro team, 3 Super Bowl rings, and 1 championship game MVP Award. Through his speed and desire to be the best, he has reinvented his position. He is unquestionably the greatest wide receiver of all-time.

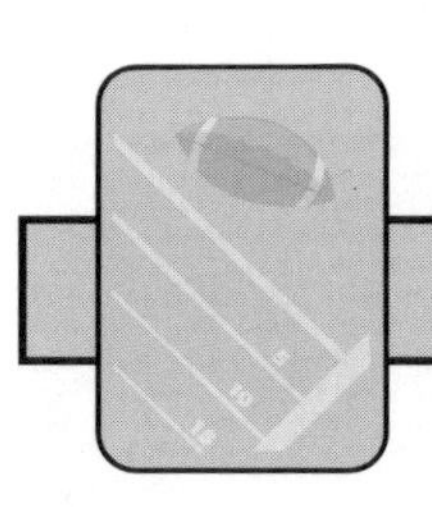

CHAPTER 8

Steve Young

Steve Young had the unenviable task of following Joe Montana as quarterback for the 49ers. He accepted the challenge and performed admirably. He established himself as, statistically, the most accurate quarterback in NFL history, winning six passing titles. Arguably the most athletic quarterback of all time, he was also a threat as a runner, with a career rushing average of nearly 6 yards per carry. Many fans, however, never forgave him for replacing the legendary Montana.

The Will to Succeed

Jon Steven Young is the great-great-great-grandson of Mormon leader Brigham Young, the second president of the Church of Jesus Christ of Latter-Day Saints and the first territorial governor of Utah. Steve was born on October 11, 1961, in Salt Lake City, Utah, the center of the Mormon faith. He was one of four sons born to LeGrande and Sherry Young. When he was a young boy, his family moved east, settling in the prosperous community of Greenwich, Connecticut. His father began practicing law, eventually becoming a New York corporate lawyer specializing in labor cases.

Statistically the most accurate passer in NFL history, Steve Young won six passing titles throughout his career.

Steve exhibited athletic ability at a very young age. Before he was three, he could dribble a basketball and do push-ups. His father, who had played football at Brigham Young University (BYU), took notice of these talents and encouraged Steve to develop them. Sports became an important part of his life.

Football quickly became his favorite pastime. In addition to playing it, he read all about the sport whenever he could. "I read all the strange football stories," he remembered, "like 'Linebackers of the NFL.' Those were my book reports from the second through the ninth grades."[116]

Steve had a burning desire to do well, a desire undoubtedly instilled in him by his father. "My dad wanted you to do everything perfectly," recalled Steve. "And he wanted to keep you humble."[117] At the same time, his parents insisted he keep up with his schoolwork. By the time he was in high school, he was both a top athlete and a top student.

At Greenwich High School, Young starred in baseball, basketball, and football. His solid work ethic was one of the things that separated him from the other kids his age. As a senior, he averaged 20 points a game in basketball and batted .600 for the baseball team.

Football, however, was his first love. Steve won the starting quarterback position as a junior. He played the position with reckless abandon, running the ball more than most quarterbacks and throwing only when necessary. "I optioned everything," said Steve. "My friends would yell, 'Pitch the ball, pitch the ball,' but I'd keep it."[118] In his senior year, he led his team all the way to the county championship game against Darien High School.

That same year, Young was named an honorable mention Prep All-America. Since he was also a member of the school's Honor Society and a National Merit Scholarship nominee, he was recruited by numerous colleges. Because of his Mormon affiliation, he decided to attend BYU, his father's alma mater.

Developing His Skills

When Young arrived at BYU as a freshman in 1980, he was the eighth quarterback ranked on the team's depth chart. Coach LaVell Edwards's Cougars featured a passing game. Since Young so rarely threw the ball in high school, his ability to do so in college was seriously questioned. It even was suggested that he switch positions to defensive back. Discouraged, Steve called home and told his father he was thinking of quitting the team. His father quickly put an end to such thoughts. "You can quit," he told his son, "but if you do, you can't live here."[119]

Young played collegiate football at Brigham Young University under coach LaVell Edwards (pictured).

In January of Young's freshman year, Ted Tollner was hired as BYU's quarterback coach. It was a move that would have a significant effect on Steve's football career. Tollner spent countless hours with him, working to improve Young's accuracy. Steve was a willing student, and by the time his sophomore season began, he had moved up to number two on the depth chart, right behind senior All-America Jim McMahon.

When McMahon suffered a knee injury in the fourth game of the year, Young got his chance to start. He made the most of it, impressing everyone with both his passing and running skills. McMahon returned three weeks later, but Young had erased any doubts that remained about his ability to run the Cougars' offense. The next year the starting job was Young's, with McMahon having moved on to the professional ranks. Young's junior season was a rousing success. He was named the Western Athletic Conference (WAC) Offensive Player of the Year as he threw for 3,100 yards and 18 touchdowns, and rushed for 407 yards himself.

It was only a hint of things to come. As a senior, Young led BYU to a 10-1 record. He completed over 70 percent of his passes, gaining 3,902 yards through the air, and ran for another 444 yards. For the year Steve set or tied thirteen NCAA records—nine for passing and four for total offense. He was a consensus All-America and runner-up in the voting for the Heisman Trophy. He was also a second-team Academic All-America. Recognized as the best college quarterback in the nation, Young's future in the professional ranks seemed assured.

The United States Football League

In 1984 the NFL faced competition for the fans' dollar from the upstart United States Football League (USFL). The Los Angeles Express of the new circuit made Young their first selection in the league's draft early that year, then offered him an incredible $40 million multiyear contract. The Cincinnati Bengals had wanted to make him the number one pick in the NFL draft but could not match the Express's offer. Young signed with Los Angeles in what eventually proved to be a poor business decision.

In twenty-five games over two years, Young played well, completing 56.4 percent of his passes for 4,102 yards and 16 touchdowns. In a game in Chicago on April 20, 1985, he became the first pro player in history to pass for 300 yards and rush for 100 in the same game. Unfortunately, the USFL folded due to financial problems after just two seasons of play. Young was released as the team attempted to cut its losses.

In the summer of 1985, the NFL held a supplemental draft of USFL players. The Tampa Bay Buccaneers selected Young and signed him to a six-year, $1.2 million contract that September. His performance with the Bucs was less than what was expected. It was not, however, entirely Young's fault. As Peter

King of *Sports Illustrated* wrote, "Young and Tampa Bay were a bad match from the start. Conservative coach Leeman Bennett had no idea how to incorporate an imaginative, free-form talent like Young into his offensive system."[120] Bennett wanted Young to be the type of passer who remained in the pocket. Unfortunately, the Bucs' offensive line was not good enough to provide him the protection this type of offense required.

With only four wins in thirty-two games over two seasons with the team, Tampa Bay traded Young to the San Francisco 49ers on April 24, 1987, in exchange for two draft picks and a reported $1 million. Steve was excited about the prospect of going from a last-place team to one that had made the playoffs the previous year. There was only one drawback. The 49ers already had the best quarterback in the game: Joe Montana. Young would join the team as his backup, at least for the immediate future.

From Backup to Starter

From 1987 to 1990, Montana continued to lead the 49ers, despite sustaining several injuries. Young appeared in thirty-five games over those four years, starting ten. He made the most of his opportunities, performing admirably when he got the chance. In his first year, he completed nearly 54 percent of his passes and threw for 10 touchdowns without a single interception. His quarterback rating of 120.8 would have been a league record had he played enough to qualify. The following season, in a game against the Minnesota Vikings, Young made a 49-yard touchdown run that was rated by NFL Films president Steve Sabol as "the best in football over the past twenty-five years."[121] In 1989 he again had a quarterback rating of 120.8.

Despite Young's performance, Montana maintained his status as San Francisco's number one quarterback. Unfortunately, the relationship between starter and understudy began to show signs of strain. At times Montana seemed to resent Young, reportedly getting upset when Steve occasionally replaced him.

The situation remained the same until just prior to the 1991 season when it was revealed that a severe elbow injury would cause Montana to miss the entire year. Thrust into the spotlight, Young came through in fine fashion. He threw for 348 yards against both the San Diego Chargers and Atlanta Falcons and completed an amazing 18 of 20 passes against the Detroit Lions. A knee injury interrupted Young's run, but he returned in the final game of the year. He ended the season on a high note, leading the 49ers to a 52–14 win over the Chicago Bears. Coach George Seifert considered the game a turning point in Young's career. "Before that game," said Seifert, "Steve had played very well, but many times he seemed to be struggling almost as if he were fighting with himself. I told him to just move the club and not worry about how he had to do it. I said, 'You have God-given abilities. Just take advantage of them.'"[122]

Young agreed with his coach's assessment of the situation. "I came back for the last game of the 1991 season much more at peace with myself about everything," he said. "I knew I had to relax

From the ground, Steve Young watches as Jerry Rice catches one of Young's 18 completed passes.

Young laid the ball where only Rice (80) could reach it in his second game against the Atlanta Falcons.

more and let everything come together. I decided I just had to be me and play ball."[123]

For the year Young completed 64.5 percent of his passes for 2,517 yards and 17 touchdowns. He also ran for 4 touchdowns. The

49ers, however, came up short of the playoffs with a 10-6 mark. Despite his solid season, many observers pointed to his failure to lead San Francisco to the playoffs as proof that Young was not a capable successor to Montana.

Young shook off the criticism and bounced back to have an outstanding year in 1992. With Montana still unable to play until the last week of the regular season, Young guided the team to an NFL-best 14-2 record and a spot in the playoffs. He again led the league's quarterbacks with a rating of 107. In doing so, he became the first quarterback in history to record over 100 in successive seasons. His pass-completion percentage of 66.7 also led the league (the fourth straight season he completed over 60 percent of his attempts), as did his 25 touchdown passes. In addition, he averaged 7.1 yards per carry on each of his 76 rushes.

After defeating the Washington Redskins in the opening round of the playoffs, the 49ers lost to the Dallas Cowboys in the NFC Championship game. However, for his stellar performance, Young was named the NFL's Most Valuable Player of 1992. He also received the 49ers' prestigious Len Eshmont Award for "inspirational and courageous play."[124]

With Montana now recovered from his elbow injury, a quarterback controversy again loomed on the horizon. The question of who would be the starter was answered the next spring when Montana signed with the Kansas City Chiefs. The 49ers' starting job was now Young's, for better or worse.

The 1993 season began in an inauspicious way for Young. He suffered a hairline fracture of his left thumb during a preseason game against the Los Angeles Raiders. He recovered in time to start the regular season opener, but the thumb continued to bother him for several weeks. His performance did not reflect it, however. For the third straight year, Young led the NFC in passing with a rating of better than 100. He threw for more than 4,000 yards, something Montana had never accomplished. He also set a team record by throwing 183 consecutive passes without an interception.

Unfortunately, the 49ers struggled on defense. They won their division with a 10-6 record and rolled over the New York Giants, 44–3, in the divisional playoff game. When it came to the NFC title game, however, they met their match. The Dallas Cowboys sacked Young four times en route to a 38–21 victory. Young and the 49ers had come up short of a championship once again.

A Storybook Season

Despite three solid years at quarterback, Young was still not accepted by a large portion of the 49er fan base. As good as he had been, he could never replace Montana in the hearts of many fans. He had not yet led the team to the Super Bowl. However, that would all change in 1994.

The season began with San Francisco winning three of its first four games and Young throwing for about 300 yards per contest. The next week, however, against Philadelphia, the 49ers couldn't do anything right as the Eagles opened up a commanding 40–8 lead. Late in the second half, Coach Seifert sent Young to the bench. Uncharacteristically, Young exploded upon reaching the sideline. He told Seifert he was embarrassed at being removed and was

Leading the 49ers rushing game, Young dodges a San Diego defender in Super Bowl XXIX.

tired of being made to look like a scapegoat. "I took it the wrong way," said Young.

> I reacted to what happened and the whole day. I'll probably never scream at a coach again, but I felt good about it then. By the end of the fourth quarter, the fans were upset, we were upset. We were all kind of wondering, "How good are we?" We were touted as this great team, but obviously there was a lot of work to be done. Looking back, that humiliation was one of the most important things that happened all season.[125]

Although the Eagles won the game, Young had grown in the eyes of his teammates, becoming one of the guys by taking on the coach. The next day Seifert apologized for handling the situation the way he did.

There was no longer any question concerning Young's ability to lead the team. He guided the 49ers to a 13-3 record and another Western Division crown. He extended his record by winning a fourth straight passing title, this time with a new NFL-record rating of 112.8. Young set new 49er marks for completion percentage (70.3) and touchdown passes (35). For his spectacular performance, he won his second Most Valuable Player trophy.

San Francisco made it to the Super Bowl under Young's leadership for the first time, defeating the Chicago Bears in the divisional playoff and the Cowboys in the NFC title game. Their opponent in Super Bowl XXIX in January 1995 was the San Diego Chargers.

Young showed the Chargers what they were in for by hitting Jerry Rice on a 44-yard scoring pass on the opening drive of the game. By halftime he had thrown for 3 more touchdowns, giving the 49ers a 28–10 lead. At the end of the game, the 49ers had their record fifth Super Bowl victory. Young completed 24 of 36 passes for 325 yards and 6 touchdowns, surpassing Montana's old Super Bowl record of 5. He was also the game's leading rusher with 49 yards on 5 carries. San Diego coach Bobby Ross praised Young after the game. "You think you have everything else defensed, and then he breaks loose," said Ross. "You can't defense his running."[126] Young had finally managed to escape from the shadow of his famous predecessor.

Young in Charge

Over the next four seasons, Young compiled solid statistics and set several records. He won two more league passing titles (1996, 1997), giving him six to tie the NFL mark. He broke Montana's records by throwing touchdown passes in eighteen consecutive games and by recording six consecutive games of 300 or more yards passing (1998). The 49ers reached the playoffs in each of the four years but never made it back to the Super Bowl.

San Francisco started the 1999 season by splitting its first two games. Young, however, was taking a beating physically. The offensive line was inexperienced and couldn't provide him with the necessary protection. In addition, with running back Garrison Hearst out of action following surgery, opposing defenses were focusing on Young.

In the third game of the year, Arizona Cardinals cornerback Aenas Williams sacked Young on a blindside blitz just before halftime. The quarterback was knocked to the turf and hit his head against teammate Dave Fiore's helmet. He was unconscious for about half a minute and had to leave the game with a concussion.

It was later revealed that Young had also suffered a concussion the week before against New Orleans. Because of the double concussion, doctors suggested he sit out the remainder of the season for health reasons. Without Young, the 49ers won just one of their last twelve games. Steve was urged by friends and family to retire but hesitated to make such a decision knowing his importance to the team. Early the next June, however, he made it official. Young was walking away from football after fifteen seasons in the NFL. "It was a tough decision," said Young, "but I know that I've made the right one and I really felt it was right in my heart. I go forward and feel thrilled for what lies ahead of me. But at the same time it is sad to end an era that meant so much to me. I loved playing for the San Francisco 49ers."[127]

Walking Away

Much of Young's postplaying career time is spent managing numerous youth-oriented organizations, including his Forever Young Foundation [FYF]. This nonprofit foundation focuses on the development and education of children. The charity distributes funds through community outreach programs that provide academic, therapeutic, and athletic opportunities to underprivileged and seriously ill youths. In addition to his work with FYF, Young has received his law degree from BYU, is the cofounder of a Salt Lake City–based Internet company, and is considering starting a venture capital firm.

Young joined the 49ers in the unenviable position of having to succeed a Hall of Famer. He persevered and left the game as the

Steve Young hugs the Vince Lombardi trophy. Under his leadership, the San Francisco 49ers defeat the San Diego Chargers in Super Bowl XXIX.

highest-rated quarterback in NFL history. He is also the most accurate, having completed 64.2 percent of his throws. As lethal a rusher as he was a thrower, Young is the second-leading all-time ground gainer among quarterbacks, trailing only Randall Cunningham with 4,239 yards. He left the game he loved with two NFL Most Valuable Player Awards, seven selections to the Pro Bowl, and cer-

After an injury-ridden career, Steve Young retires from the 49ers in 1999.

Steve and Barbara Young watch as the San Francisco 49ers retire his number 8 jersey for being one of the league's most talented leaders.

tain election to the Pro Football Hall of Fame when he becomes eligible.

Young received the ultimate tribute from NFL Commissioner Paul Tagliabue.

> Steve Young is the personification of what an NFL player should be. On the field, he was one of the league's most gifted athletes and tenacious leaders. His enthusiasm for the game brought joy to football fans everywhere. He will no doubt go down as one of the greatest quarterbacks in history.

And his work off the field has been just as impressive. From earning his law degree to his work with children through the Forever Young foundation, Steve's accomplishments as a community leader set a standard for all of us to admire. As Commissioner and as a fan, I say thank you to Steve Young.[128]

Notes

Chapter 1: Excitement Personified

1. Quoted in Carl Nolte, "The 49ers at 50," *SFGate*. www.sfgate.com/cgi-bin/article.cti?file=/chronicle/archive/1996/12/09/SP39PG1.DTL.
2. Quoted in Nolte, "The 49ers at 50."
3. Quoted in Joseph Hession, *Forty Niners: Looking Back*. San Francisco: Foghorn Press, 1986, p. 7.
4. Quoted in Hession, *Forty Niners*, p. 30.

Chapter 2: Joe Perry

5. Quoted in Dave Newhouse, *The Million Dollar Backfield*. Berkeley, CA: Frog, Ltd., Books, 2000, p. 11.
6. Quoted in Newhouse, *The Million Dollar Backfield*, p. 13.
7. Quoted in Newhouse, *The Million Dollar Backfield*, p. 17.
8. Quoted in Newhouse, *The Million Dollar Backfield*, p. 20.
9. Quoted in Hession, *Forty Niners*, p. 52.
10. Quoted in Newhouse, *The Million Dollar Backfield*, p. 3.
11. Quoted in Hession, *Forty Niners*, p. 52.
12. Quoted in Newhouse, *The Million Dollar Backfield*, p. 5.
13. Quoted in Hession, *Forty Niners*, p. 34.
14. Quoted in Steve Cassady, "Heroes but Not Champions," *Sports History*, November 1988, p. 37.
15. Quoted in Newhouse, *The Million Dollar Backfield*, p. 31.
16. Quoted in Newhouse, *The Million Dollar Backfield*, p. 33.
17. Quoted in Newhouse, *The Million Dollar Backfield*, p. 35.
18. Quoted in Newhouse, *The Million Dollar Backfield*, p. 36.
19. Quoted in Newhouse, *The Million Dollar Backfield*, p. 36.
20. Quoted in Newhouse, *The Million Dollar Backfield*, p. 39.
21. Quoted in Ronald L. Mendell and Timothy B. Phares, *Who's Who in Football*. New Rochelle, NY: Arlington House, 1974, p. 270.
22. Quoted in Newhouse, *The Million Dollar Backfield*, pp. 39–40.
23. Quoted in Newhouse, *The Million Dollar Backfield*, p. 40.
24. Quoted in Hession, *Forty Niners*, p. 52.

Chapter 3: Hugh McElhenny

25. Quoted in Cassady, "Heroes but Not Champions," p. 39.
26. Quoted in Newhouse, *The Million Dollar Backfield*, p. 57.
27. Quoted in Newhouse, *The Million Dollar Backfield*, p. 57.
28. Quoted in Newhouse, *The Million Dollar Backfield*, p. 58.
29. Quoted in Newhouse, *The Million Dollar Backfield*, p. 58.
30. Quoted in Newhouse, *The Million Dollar Backfield*, p. 59.
31. Quoted in Newhouse, *The Million Dollar Backfield*, p. 60.
32. Quoted in Newhouse, *The Million Dollar Backfield*, p. 64.
33. Quoted in Bob Carroll et al., eds., *Total Football*. New York: HarperCollins, 1997, p. 263.
34. Quoted in Hession, *Forty Niners*, p. 34.
35. Quoted in Hession, *Forty Niners*, p. 33.
36. Quoted in Hession, *Forty Niners*, p. 33.
37. Quoted in Newhouse, *The Million Dollar Backfield*, p. 68.
38. Quoted in Newhouse, *The Million Dollar Backfield*, p. 69.
39. Quoted in Newhouse, *The Million Dollar Backfield*, p. 71.
40. Quoted in Newhouse, *The Million Dollar Backfield*, p. 74.
41. Quoted in Newhouse, *The Million Dollar Backfield*, p. 77.
42. Quoted in Newhouse, *The Million Dollar Backfield*, pp. 49, 82
43. Quoted in Newhouse, *The Million Dollar Backfield*, p. 86.
44. Quoted in Newhouse, *The Million Dollar Backfield*, p. 87.
45. Quoted in Jim Gehman, "Where Are They Now: Hugh McElhenny," *NFL*. www.nfl.com/news/Wherenow/mcelhenny.html.
46. Quoted in Newhouse, *The Million Dollar Backfield*, p. 88.

Chapter 4: Bill Walsh

47. Quoted in Art Spander, "Walsh Molded Mediocrity into Champions," *The Sporting News*, February 6, 1989, p. 7.
48. Quoted in Art Spander, "Bill Walsh—No. 6," *Inside Bay Area*. www.celebrate2000-ang.com/sportsfigures.asp?Sports=Bill_Walsh.
49. Quoted in Frank Cooney, "Football's Master Strategist Bill Walsh," *The Sporting News 1985 Pro Football Yearbook*, p. 14.
50. Quoted in Spander, "Bill Walsh—No. 6."
51. Quoted in Charles Moritz, ed., *Current Biography Yearbook: 1989*. New York: H. W. Wilson, 1989, p. 602.
52. Quoted in Moritz, *Current Biography Yearbook: 1989*, p. 603.
53. Quoted in Moritz, *Current Biography Yearbook: 1989*, p. 603.
54. Quoted in Cooney, "Football's Master Strategist Bill Walsh," p. 13.

55. Quoted in Cooney, "Football's Master Strategist Bill Walsh," p. 13.
56. Quoted in Moritz, *Current Biography Yearbook: 1989*, p. 603.
57. Quoted in Moritz, *Current Biography Yearbook: 1989*, p. 604.
58. Quoted in Glenn Dickey, *Glenn Dickey's 49ers*. Roseville, CA: Prima Publishing, 2000, p. 16.
59. Quoted in Moritz, *Current Biography Yearbook: 1989*, p. 604.
60. Quoted in Cooney, "Football's Master Strategist Bill Walsh," p. 16.
61. Quoted in Dickey, *Glenn Dickey's 49ers*, p. 83.
62. Quoted in Moritz, *Current Biography Yearbook: 1989*, p. 606.
63. Quoted in Dickey, *Glenn Dickey's 49ers*, p. 206.
64. Quoted in Spander, "Bill Walsh—No. 6."

Chapter 5: Joe Montana

65. Quoted in Larry Schwartz, "No Ordinary Joe," *ESPN*. espn.go.com/classic/biography/s/montana_joe.html.
66. Quoted in Schwartz, "No Ordinary Joe."
67. Quoted in Schwartz, "No Ordinary Joe."
68. Quoted in Steve Wulf, "The Passing of an Era," *Time*. www.time.com/time/magazine/archive/1995/950424/950424.sport.html.
69. Quoted in Glenn Dickey, "Bill Walsh's Big Role in Montana's Greatness," *SFGate*. www.sfgate.com/cgi-bin/article.cgi?file=/chronicle/archive/1997/12/15/SP68440.DTL&type=printable.
70. Quoted in Hession, *Forty Niners*, p. 138.
71. Quoted in Bob McCoy, ed., *The Sporting News Super Bowl Book 1987 Edition*. St. Louis: The Sporting News, 1987, p. 192.
72. Quoted in Ira Miller, "Duel with Marino Tops the List," *SFGate*. www.sfgate.com/cgi-bin/article.cgi?file=/chronicle/archive/1997/12/15/SP30217.DTL&type=printable.
73. Quoted in Jonathan Curiel, "Super Four," *SFGate*. www.sfgate.com/cgi-bin/article.cgi?file=/chronicle/archive/1997/12/15/SP4985.DTL&type=printable.
74. Quoted in Dickey, *Glenn Dickey's 49ers*, p. 99.
75. Quoted in Scott Ostler, "Joe Montana Picks His Favorites," *NFL*. www.nfl.com/news/hof/80s/montana.html.
76. Quoted in Dickey, *Glenn Dickey's 49ers*, p. 147.
77. Quoted in Ira Miller, "He's Back in the Big Picture," *SFGate*. www.sfgate.com/cgi-bin/article.cgi?file=/chronicle/archive/1997/12/15/SP18334.DTL&type=printable.

Chapter 6: Ronnie Lott

78. Quoted in Carroll, *Total Football*, p. 259.
79. Quoted in Judith Graham, ed., *Current Biography Yearbook: 1994*. New York: H. W. Wilson, 1994, p. 343.
80. Quoted in Jill Lieber, "Hitter with Heart," *Sports Illustrated*, January 23, 1989, p. 47.
81. Quoted in Lieber, "Hitter with Heart," p. 47.
82. Quoted in Graham, *Current Biography Yearbook: 1994*, p. 343.
83. Quoted in Graham, *Current Biography Yearbook: 1994*, p. 343.
84. Quoted in Hession, *Forty Niners*, p. 132.
85. Quoted in Hession, *Forty Niners*, p. 132.
86. Quoted in Graham, *Current Biography Yearbook: 1994*, p. 344.
87. Quoted in Graham, *Current Biography Yearbook: 1994*, p. 344.
88. Quoted in Lieber, "Hitter with Heart," p. 46.
89. Quoted in James Buckley Jr., "Super Bowl Tough Guys," *Sports Illustrated*, December 25, 2000–January 1, 2001, p. 38.
90. Quoted in Graham, *Current Biography Yearbook: 1994*, p. 344.
91. Quoted in Graham, *Current Biography Yearbook: 1994*, p. 344.
92. Quoted in Jerry McDonald, "A Whole Lott of Great Football," *Inside Bay Area*. www.celebrate2000-ang.com/sportsfigures.asp?Sports=Ronnie_Lott.
93. Quoted in Graham, *Current Biography Yearbook: 1994*, p. 345.
94. Quoted in Graham, *Current Biography Yearbook: 1994*, p. 345.
95. Quoted in *Jet*, "Ronnie Lott Inducted into Pro Football Hall of Fame," August 14, 2000. www.findarticles.com/cf_0/m1355/10_98/64426273/p1/article.jhtml?term=%22Ronnie+Lott%22.

Chapter 7: Jerry Rice

96. Quoted in Monte Poole, "Jerry Rice—No. 8," *Inside Bay Area*. www.celebrate2000-ang.com/sportsfigures.asp?Sports=Jerry_Rice.
97. Quoted in Poole, "Jerry Rice—No. 8."
98. Quoted in Charles Moritz, ed., *Current Biography Yearbook: 1990*. New York: H. W. Wilson, 1990, p. 525.
99. Quoted in Bob Carter, "49ers Era Was Rice Era," *ESPN*. espn.go.com/classic/biography/s/Rice_Jerry.html.
100. Quoted in Carroll, *Total Football*, p. 272.
101. Quoted in Brian Murphy, "Rice Driven to Be Better than Best," *Press Democrat*. www.pressdemo.com/49ers/rice.html.
102. Quoted in Moritz, *Current Biography Yearbook: 1990*, p. 525.
103. Quoted in Moritz, *Current Biography Yearbook: 1990*, p. 525.

104. Quoted in Moritz, *Current Biography Yearbook: 1990*, p. 525.
105. Quoted in Moritz, *Current Biography Yearbook: 1990*, pp. 525, 526.
106. Quoted in Moritz, *Current Biography Yearbook: 1990*, p. 526.
107. Quoted in Moritz, *Current Biography Yearbook: 1990*, p. 526.
108. Quoted in Moritz, *Current Biography Yearbook: 1990*, p. 526.
109. Quoted in Moritz, *Current Biography Yearbook: 1990*, p. 527.
110. Quoted in Murphy, "Rice Driven to Be Better than Best."
111. Quoted in Moritz, *Current Biography Yearbook: 1990*, p. 527.
112. Quoted in Moritz, *Current Biography Yearbook: 1990*, p. 527.
113. Quoted in Moritz, *Current Biography Yearbook: 1990*, p. 527.
114. Quoted in Carter, "49ers Era Was Rice Era."
115. Quoted in Nancy Gay, "Middle Man," *NFL*. www.nfl.com/49ers/news/001031rice.html.

Chapter 8: Steve Young

116. Quoted in Dave Newhouse, "49ers QB Runs with an Elite Crowd," *Inside Bay Area*. www.celebrate2000-ang.com/sportsfigures.asp?Sports=Steve_Young.
117. Quoted in Judith Graham, ed., *Current Biography Yearbook: 1993*. New York: H. W. Wilson, 1993, p. 612.
118. Quoted in Newhouse, "49ers QB Runs with an Elite Crowd."
119. Quoted in Graham, *Current Biography Yearbook: 1993*, p. 612.
120. Quoted in Graham, *Current Biography Yearbook: 1993*, p. 613.
121. Quoted in Graham, *Current Biography Yearbook: 1993*, p. 613.
122. Quoted in Graham, *Current Biography Yearbook: 1993*, p. 614.
123. Quoted in Graham, *Current Biography Yearbook: 1993*, p. 614.
124. Quoted in Graham, *Current Biography Yearbook: 1993*, p. 614.
125. Quoted in Barry M. Bloom, "Super Steve," *Sport*, September 1995, p. 43.
126. Quoted in Dickey, *Glenn Dickey's 49ers*, p. 158.
127. Quoted in *NFL*, "Young Ends 15-Year Career." www.nfl.com/49ers/young/retirement.html.
128. Quoted in *NFL*, "Commissioner: Steve Set a Standard," www.nfl.com/49ers/young/tagliabue.html.

For Further Reading

Books

Gene Brown, ed., *The New York Times Encyclopedia of Sports—Football*. New York: Arno Press, 1979. A collection of articles from the *New York Times* tracing the history of football from 1905 to 1979.

Bob Carroll, *100 Greatest Running Backs*. New York: Crescent Books, 1989. Looks at the players who grind out the yards and put points on the board.

Peter King, *Football: A History of the Professional Game*. New York: Time, 1996. Sports Illustrated series volume that is an authoritative tribute to America's most popular sport.

Howie Long, *Football for Dummies*. New York: Hungry Minds, 1998. This volume in the For Dummies series examines every aspect of football, including plays, positions, and strategy.

Joe Montana with Richard Weiner, *Joe Montana's Art and Magic of Quarterbacking*. New York: Henry Holt, 1997. The 49er Hall of Fame quarterback reveals what makes a quarterback successful, from the fundamentals through the intangibles.

National Football League, *The Official NFL 2001 Record and Fact Book*. New York: Workman Publishing, 2001. This all-in-one resourse of statistics, information, and trivia is the only record book authorized by the NFL.

Bill Walsh with Brian Billick and Jim Peterson, *Bill Walsh: Finding the Winning Edge*. Champaign, IL: Sports Publishing, 1997. An inside look at the tenure of football's top coaches with one of the era's most dominating professional football teams.

Richard Whittingham, *The Fireside Book of Pro Football*. New York: Simon & Schuster, 1989. Collection of writings on professional football.

Works Consulted

Books

Bob Carroll et al., eds., *Total Football*. New York: HarperCollins, 1997. Comprehensive football reference containing statistics and historical essays.

Glenn Dickey, *Glenn Dickey's 49ers*. Roseville, CA: Prima Publishing, 2000. Dickey's book chronicles the rise, fall, and rebirth of the NFL's greatest dynasty.

Judith Graham, ed., *Current Biography Yearbook: 1993*. New York: H. W. Wilson, 1993. Library volume that contains all the biographies published in the eleven 1993 issues of *Current Biography Magazine.*

———, *Current Biography Yearbook: 1994*. New York: H. W. Wilson, 1994. Library volume that contains all the biographies published in the eleven 1994 issues of *Current Biography Magazine.*

Joseph Hession, *Forty Niners: Looking Back*. San Francisco: Foghorn Press, 1986. This book covers the history of the 49ers from the team's inception up through the 1980s. In addition to short biographical sketches of many players, it includes a thorough records section.

Bob McCoy, ed., *The Sporting News Super Bowl Book 1987 Edition*. St. Louis: The Sporting News, 1987. This annual guide published by *The Sporting News* has articles, facts, and figures on each of the first twenty Super Bowls.

Ronald L. Mendell and Timothy B. Phares, *Who's Who in Football.* New Rochelle, NY: Arlington House, 1974. Profiles more than 1,400 football personalities from the game's birth through 1973.

Charles Moritz, ed., *Current Biography Yearbook: 1983*. New York: H. W. Wilson, 1983. The 1983 volume in the *Current Biography Magazine.*

———, *Current Biography Yearbook: 1989*. New York: H. W. Wilson, 1989. The 1989 volume in the *Current Biography Magazine.*

———, *Current Biography Yearbook: 1990*. New York: H. W. Wilson, 1990. The 1990 volume in the *Current Biography Magazine.*

Dave Newhouse, *The Million Dollar Backfield*. Berkeley, CA: Frog, Ltd., Books, 2000. An in-depth look at Y. A. Tittle, Joe Perry, Hugh McElhenny, and John Henry Johnson, the four men who composed the San Francisco 49ers' backfield in the 1950s.

Periodicals

Barry M. Bloom, "Super Steve," *Sport*, September 1995.

James Buckley Jr., "Super Bowl Tough Guys," *Sports Illustrated,* December 25, 2000–January 1, 2001.

Steve Cassady, "Heroes but Not Champions," *Sports History,* November 1988.

Frank Cooney, "Football's Master Strategist Bill Walsh," *The Sporting News 1985 Pro Football Yearbook.*

Jill Lieber, "Hitter with Heart," *Sports Illustrated*, January 23, 1989.

Art Spander, "Walsh Molded Mediocrity into Champions," *The Sporting News*, February 6, 1989.

Internet Sources

Bob Carter, "49ers Era Was Rice Era," ESPN. espn.go.com/classic/biography/s/Rice_Jerry.html.

Jonathan Curiel, "Super Four," *SFGate.* www.sfgate.com/cgi-bin/article.cgi?file=/chronicle/archive/1997/12/15/SP4985.DTL&type=printable.

Glenn Dickey, "Bill Walsh's Big Role in Montana's Greatness," *SFGate.* www.sfgate.com/cgi-bin/article.cgi?file=/chronicle/archive/1997/12/15/SP68440.DTL&type=printable.

Nancy Gay, "Middle Man," *NFL.* www.nfl.com/49ers/news/001031rice.html.

Jim Gehman, "Where Are They Now: Hugh McElhenny," NFL. www.nfl.com/news/Wherenow/mcelhenny.html.

Jet, "Ronnie Lott Inducted into Pro Football Hall of Fame," August 14, 2000. www.findarticles.com/cf_0/m1355/10_98/64426273/p1/article.jhtml?term=%22Ronnie+Lott%22.

Jerry McDonald, "A Whole Lott of Great Football," *Inside Bay Area*, www.celebrate2000-ang.com/sportsfigures.asp?Sports=Ronnie_Lott.

Ira Miller, "Duel with Marino Tops the List," *SFGate*. www.sfgate.com/cgi-bin/article.cgi?file=/chronicle/archive/1997/12/15/SP30217.DTL&type=printable.

———, "He's Back in the Big Picture," *SFGate*. www.sfgate.com/cgi-bin/article.cgi?file=/chronicle/archive/1997/12/15/SP18334.DTL&type=printable.

Brian Murphy, "Rice Driven to Be Better than Best," *Press Democrat*. www.pressdemo.com/49ers/rice.html.

Dave Newhouse, "49ers QB Runs with an Elite Crowd," *Inside Bay Area*. www.celebrate2000-ang.com/sportsfigures.asp?Sports=Steve_Young.

NFL, "Commissioner: Steve Set a Standard." www.nfl.com/49ers/young/tagliabue.html.

———, "Young Ends 15-Year Career." www.nfl.com/49ers/young/retirement.html.

Carl Nolte, "The 49ers at 50," *SFGate*. www.sfgate.com/cgi-bin/article.cti?file=/chronicle/archive/1996/12/09/SP39PG1.DTL.

Scott Ostler, "Joe Montana Picks His Favorites," *NFL*. www.nfl.com/news/hof/80s/montana.html.

Monte Poole, "Jerry Rice—No. 8," *Inside Bay Area*. www.celebrate2000-ang.com/sportsfigures.asp?Sports=Jerry_Rice.

Larry Schwartz, "No Ordinary Joe," ESPN. espn.go.com/classic/biography/s/montana_joe.html.

Art Spander, "Bill Walsh—No. 6," *Inside Bay Area*. www.celebrate2000-ang.com/sportsfigures.asp?Sports=Bill_Walsh.

Steve Wulf, "The Passing of an Era," *Time*. www.time.com/time/magazine/archive/1995/950424/950424.sport.html.

Index

Picture Credits

Cover Photo: © Craig Jones/Allsport
© AFP/CORBIS, 70, 96, 101, 109
Allsport USA/Allsport, 73
Associated Press AP, 20, 29, 42, 50, 57, 60, 62, 68, 76, 78, 87, 90, 98, 102, 107
Associated Press AP/DALLAS MORNING NEWS, 64
© Bettmann/CORBIS, 9, 13, 15, 18, 25, 30, 33, 36, 39, 45, 55
Jonathan Daniel/Allsport, 93
Otto Greule/Allsport, 53
Will Hart/Allsport, 48
Doug Pensinger/Allsport, 22
Mike Powell/Allsport, 104
© Reuters NewMedia Inc./CORBIS, 81, 84, 108

About the Author

John F. Grabowski is a native of Brooklyn, New York. He holds a bachelor's degree in psychology from City College of New York and a master's degree in educational psychology from Teacher's College, Columbia University. He has been a teacher for thirty-one years as well as a freelance writer, specializing in the fields of sports, education, and comedy. His body of published work includes thirty books; a nationally syndicated sports column; consultation on several math textbooks; articles for newspapers, magazines, and the programs of professional sports teams; and comedy material sold to Jay Leno, Joan Rivers, Yakov Smirnoff, and numerous other comics. He and his wife, Patricia, live in Staten Island with their daughter, Elizabeth.